INSURRECTION

The 1967 Plainfield City Riot
and the
Plainfield High School
Racial Disturbance of 1969

A personal recollection
of those two tragic events

BY ISAIAH TREMAINE

ISBN:1546775951
ISBN-13:9781546775959

DEDICATION

To all those who still love the city
of
Plainfield, New Jersey

ACKNOWLEDGMENTS

My sincere thanks to

PAUL GRZELLA
General Manager/Editor
The Courier News

SARAH HULL
Archivist
Plainfield Public Library

**THE AMERICAN CIVIL LIBERTIES UNION
OF NEW JERSEY**

DANIEL J. TURKEL
For his spirited input during final reviews of the
story

JACKJAYdigital
For his cover design

GOOGLE MAPS

And
JOSEPH POTTACKAL
For his skilled and insightful editing

.

INTRODUCTION

I should have written this book long ago... I certainly wanted to. But I have delayed, avoided, and procrastinated for years when it came to engaging the subject of the Plainfield city riot of 1967 and the high school disturbances of 1969.

Why?

My simple answer—they have been too painful to recount.

It's not that they aren't interesting stories. They both have excitement and tragedy and are absolutely true events. And they both changed my hometown of Plainfield forever. However, when writing a book, you stay with the subject for hours, weeks, months, even years. To be locked into such heartbreak for so long, well, was just not appealing.

July 2017 will mark fifty years since the city riot.

While I still have all my faculties and I can recall most everything in detail, I felt it was actually my duty to get the story finally recorded—at least my version of what happened. Although it is an account from my perspective (an Afro-American male), I promise that every event recalled actually happened. I have verified my recollections with existing historical records; this final version is as accurate as I can make it.

Most importantly, I will also try to take you back to the time and emotion of the era. Plainfield had been nicknamed "the Queen City" and it deserved the title for the longest time. Although the riots almost destroyed the Queen City, it survived. Plainfield endured because those who loved the city stayed and fought for its survival.

To those hearty Plainfielders, I dedicate this book.

1 "A TERRIFIC TOWN"

The City of Plainfield has been around for a long time. It was originally settled by the Quakers in 1684. In the beginning, the small area that was known as Plainfield village was actually part of the Westfield community. By 1869, one hundred eighty-five years after its founding, Plainfield had grown large enough to stand on its own and become an official city.

The city's growth continued. Larger and more sophisticated businesses moved to Plainfield including clothes makers, chemical producers, and eventually truck makers. At the same time, the city was gaining a reputation as a "resort" location. Soon many wealthy people preferred Plainfield over the heat and hubbub of New York City. They traveled by train to the beauty and tranquility the city offered. The Sleepy Hollow area of Plainfield, with its exquisite homes, started during that period. To protect those mansions and all the homes in Plainfield, a well-staffed police department and the only paid fire department in the area were created.

The Plainfield Courier News, Central Jersey's largest newspaper at the time, was headquartered in Plainfield. The city also boasted a highly ranked public school system and two excellent private schools—the Wardlaw Country Day School for boys and the Hartridge School for girls.

A pride of Plainfield was its large and established downtown business and shopping stores that were, by far, the best in the area. Shoppers from North and South Plainfield, Piscataway, Dunellen, Greenbrook, Watchung, Warren, Scotch Plains, Fanwood, and Edison supported Plainfield's elegant business district. Downtown Plainfield featured the finest of furriers, jewelers, four movie theaters, and prominent department stores. The business owners even had television celebrities come to promote their stores. I recall noted personality Cliff Arquette came to Plainfield as his famous character Charlie Weaver to help open a new toy store. I remember Chuck McCann, who had a popular TV show on WPIX Channel 11, came to Plainfield on the day after Thanksgiving (it wasn't called Black Friday back then) as his character Little Orphan Annie to help launch the Christmas buying season. Earlier on that same Friday, Santa Claus arrived by helicopter in

Plainfield. He left the copter and was mounted on a fire engine and paraded through the downtown area to the cheers of thousands of boys and girls who came to see him. As a teenager, I would bring my baby brother and sister to see the spectacle. Santa's helicopter landed in what was the Bamberger Department store parking lot on the corner of Front Street and Roosevelt Avenue. Bamberger's later became a popular Macy's. That location is now "Supremo" Plainfield Plaza.

Of the ten communities that I mentioned, Plainfield was the only one to have a medical center. Muhlenberg Hospital had serviced Plainfield and the Central Jersey area since 1877. Leading to the hospital's Park Avenue location were dozens of doctor's offices. The best doctors in every specialty could be found there. That Park Avenue strip soon became known as "Doctor's Row" (I'll tell you what happened to Doctor's Row later in the book).

By the 1950s, all of the important structures in Plainfield, from City Hall to the YMCA building, the police station to Plainfield High school, the Courier News building to the National Guard armory on Seventh Street, were all beautifully-designed, expensive brick buildings. Among the many churches in the city, the Grace Episcopal Church, the Seventh Day Adventist Church, and the large Crescent Avenue Presbyterian Church were majestic stone structures.

A Quaker meeting house built in 1788 and the Drake House, where General George Washington stayed during the Battle of Short Hills in June 1777, are still open and active venues in Plainfield.

Plainfield has two large parks equipped with baseball diamonds and tennis and basketball courts. The internationally famous composer and conductor John Phillip Sousa held a concert in one of the city's picturesque parks.

From that rich nest of culture, wealth, and capability came several notable people. Archibald Cox was a special prosecutor selected to handle tribunals in the Watergate break-in and related criminal activity during the Nixon administration; Mr. Cox was born in Plainfield. Olympic Decathlon gold medal champion Milt Campbell was from Plainfield; he was the first African-American to win that decathlon title. Joe Black, the first black Major League Baseball pitcher to win a game in the World Series, was also from Plainfield. So was Jeff Torborg, who was a coach and a player in Major League Baseball. And NFL running back Vic Washington, who played for the San Francisco 49ers, was yet another famous person from Plainfield.

Plainfield was the birthplace of the music known as "P-Funk." George Clinton created the musical group, The Parliaments, while working in a barber shop in Plainfield. Mr. Clinton and The

Parliaments went on to great success and national fame.

For these reasons, and many more, Plainfield was the diamond in the Central Jersey area and was eventually given the nickname of "the Queen City."

2 "A WHITE REPUBLICAN TOWN"

In the first chapter, I gave you a quick snapshot of the town I was born into. It was beautiful, established, stable, and safe. It was also mostly white and Republican in its politics. To the young people living in Plainfield now, that is probably something hard to imagine. The official record of the 2016 Clinton-Trump presidential campaign showed that the population of Plainfield voted almost 12-1 for the Democrat.

But not so in the early 1960s.

Plainfield today is a town that is mostly black and Hispanic.

But not so in the early 1960s.

The current Plainfield school system is populated almost entirely by blacks and Hispanics.

But not so in the early 1960s.

I remember my years at Barlow Elementary School on the East End of Plainfield. Ellen Rossi, Kirby Smith, Peggy Wren, Gregory Corbett, Mark Reeves, and Joey Vastino, along with most of the 25 kids in my class, were white. They lived through that period of John Kennedy, Mercury astronauts, and the Cuban Missile Crisis with me. I recall two or three other black kids, but no Hispanics in my classes. I don't believe I met a Hispanic boy or girl until I was in high school. But during that time at Barlow, no one cared about skin color. Alan Howarth was white, Allen Johnson was black; but what really mattered was that both were cool and my friends. Alan Howarth was probably middle class; he lived in a cozy home on Netherwood Avenue. His family invited me to dinner one time. I recall how neat and orderly everything was in their house. But I also remember being served food I couldn't identify. I can laugh at that now. Alan Johnson lived next door to me; his poor black family was a mirror of my own, but I felt so comfortable when I visited his place. However, it had nothing to do with race. It was just that one place was familiar and the other wasn't. Although I've noted the race of my friends, at the time, I wasn't aware of race. But I'll explain that later.

One day in the fall of 1960, all the students at Barlow were asked to stay after school. Why? Vice President Richard Nixon's motorcade was going to pass by our school, and the powers that be wanted the streets lined with happy, supportive citizens for the Vice President to see. We carried our classroom chairs to the street curb and waited for him with great anticipation.

I can't imagine that happening today. I can't imagine a Republican candidate for president, Congress, governor, or even dogcatcher coming to Plainfield asking for support.

What caused the change?

Queen City Plainfield of the early 1960s was basking in the glow of years of investment from the middle class, upper-middle class, and the wealthy of Plainfield. They were proud capitalists, and in their eyes, they had done everything they could to make Plainfield a great place to live. But Plainfield did have a growing black population that didn't share in the wealth and glory. The Plainfield Republicans had overlooked them.

Now, to be clear and fair, the Plainfield I lived in did not have the blatant and cruel segregation system of many Southern states. Not even close. But we did have problems—they were just more subtle. The management of almost every business, every political office, and every position of power and authority was held by a white person. Oh, there were one or two black police officers on a force of approximately 140, but they were never in command. There were a couple of black firefighters (one was a neighbor of mine), but they were never in command either. Among eleven elementary schools, two junior high schools, and a large central high school, there were only a few black teachers: I personally did not see one until junior high school, and I did not have one until I was in high school. There might have been a few black vice principals, but I was not aware of any black principals during my time in the Plainfield school system (however, Dr. Richard F. Neblett, a member of my future church, was the first black appointed to the Plainfield Board of Education in 1963).

This lack of black personnel in high positions was unheeded for a long time in Plainfield by the white folks. But it didn't escape the notice of many in the black neighborhoods.

I have my own theory of how this imbalance came about. I'll give you the quick version.

Right after the Civil War: think of the black and white situation in this country like a 100-yard dash at a track meet. In 1865, with slaves now freed, the starter pistol is fired and the race begins; however, white folks are already halfway down the track. White folks owned businesses, maintained colleges, and were well-established in science and engineering. Many blacks were just emerging from hundreds of years of suppression. They owned no property, had no education, were not skilled, and had racist organizations determined to get them.

By 1900, some blacks had homes, maybe a few had started businesses; but whites were far ahead with great advantages in education and financial power. They had built railroads, telephones, and cameras. Black advancement was hindered by a violent racist culture in a country that supposedly believed in "liberty and justice for all." Blacks suffered from poor schools and no economic foundation—in a nation of wealthy capitalists.

That 100-yard dash continued...

World War II: one million blacks served their country well, but they returned home to secondary status, poverty, and the same built-in racism. By the 1950s, whites had built jets, rockets, and nuclear bombs, while blacks were just starting to go to college in larger numbers and achieve a bit more of the American dream. But so many were still suffering from generations of neglect, poverty, and denial of a fair education. And occasionally, some were still being lynched.

Then a brave black lady refused to sit in the back of a bus.

Rosa Parks helped to start a true civil rights movement in the United States, and that movement was to bring hope to millions. But the track meet and the race—ah, the race—whites were still way ahead.

That's my quick explanation of how the black

situation made its way to the 1960s. During the same time period of my analogy, a historic black migration from the Southern states to the Northern states took place between 1910 and the 1960s. More than ten million African-Americans left the bigotry, danger, and lack of opportunity of the South. Of the Northern states, New Jersey received an especially high number of blacks relocating from the South. The cities of Trenton, Newark, Camden, Jersey City, and Paterson, with plenty of businesses and manufacturing, were particular magnets to those looking for hope. In time, those numbers spread out to other Jersey cities that prospered, and Plainfield was one of those cities. So blacks started moving to Plainfield; my parents were part of that South-to-North migration.

Over the years, many other black folks found their way to Plainfield in similar ways. They were not well-educated and most did not have professional careers. They were simply looking for a better life and found it in Plainfield. They weren't seeking power or authority, just a home and a job. Before long, many black families became embedded in Plainfield, and they took on the character of the community for the longest time. Black people in Plainfield supported the high school football team, went to the Fourth of July parade, and shopped at the stores in downtown Plainfield just like everyone else. But remember, Plainfield was primarily a middle, upper-middle, to wealthy town. And many of those long-term white residents had been winning their race at the American "track meet" with a tradition of being bank presidents, company owners, principals of schools, and legislators. Blacks were the janitors, garbage collectors, and manual laborers of that era. At first, there were few complaints; most were happy to have a job and a chance to raise a family (especially during the era of the baby boom) without the humiliation of a segregated society. But they had to live in a manner in which they could afford. In Plainfield, that primarily meant living in the northern sector of the West End of Plainfield. From Central Avenue to Clinton Avenue, from West Front Street to West 7th Street contained the largest concentration of black folks during the 1960s era in Plainfield. Oh, there were small pockets of black people in the East End too, but nothing in comparison to the West End. The white establishment even built low-cost housing in that area, basically, to keep black folks happy in their section of town.

So that's how many blacks got to Plainfield and established themselves. But how did blacks live in the system and culture of Plainfield circa 1960?

Well, in the West End, where most blacks lived, you would find black-owned businesses and a few black professionals serving the black community. Dr. Bomar on Spooner Avenue and Dr. Gardner on Darrow Avenue were competent, respected primary care black doctors. I can't testify about Dr. Bomar, but I know Dr. Gardner was a Republican and pretty proud of it. There were many white businesses inside the West End too. I recall mom-and-pop stores like Mignella's cleaners on West Fourth Street, just a half a block away from Dr. Bomar. And the much-loved "Franky's" general store owned by a delightful old-world Italian man and his wife. Franky had a cash register, but rarely used it. After you placed the items you wanted on his counter, he would take a pencil from behind his ear, and use a brown paper shopping bag to mark down the prices of everything you bought. He would add them right in front of you. As he placed the items in the bag, you would pay the amount. By far, the majority of Franky's customers were black. And I witnessed many times that those black customers didn't have enough money for their items. Franky would let them go with the food with an unwritten, no pressure understanding that you would pay him during the next visit. He, and other white storeowners like him, didn't do things like that out of intimidation; rather, it was out of an almost family relationship that Franky and other white folks served the black community.

Across the street from Franky's used to be a YMCA building. There was a huge brick YMCA building about a mile away on Watchung Avenue in Plainfield. But for many decades, it was "understood" that that building was for white men and boys. The wooden Moorland branch YMCA across from Franky's was a bit more family oriented and a social center for the black community in that West End. Unfortunately, the old Moorland building burned down in the late 50s—I actually saw the spectacular fire from my house a block away. It was quickly replaced with a big new modern building. But it was no longer a YMCA; it converted to an independent organization and was named the "Neighborhood House." It became an even more important cultural center for the black community.

There were barbers, garages, beauty parlors, drug stores, appliance stores, undertakers, small clothing stores, places to eat, even a local branch of the fire department, all in the West End of Plainfield. And there was something else in that West End: a genuine sense of security. From the time I was five years old, my mother allowed me to roam anywhere in my neighborhood without any real concern. Everyone knew everyone else, and they watched out for each other.

The East End was safe too. We lived on that side of town for about four years before moving back to the West Side. Our home was on a small dead end street, along with six other families—all were black. But unlike the West End, that street was surrounded by a white community. There was the Irish-themed "Connor's" supermarket on the corner of East Second Street and Garwood Avenue;

it was one of the best supermarkets in Plainfield and welcomed everyone. There were other positive features of the East End: a branch of the Plainfield library, better schools, even automatic milk machines conveniently located on street corners in the neighborhood. But the real difference was the large number of white folks in the overall community. All were very friendly to me and I felt safe, but it didn't have that West End feel in which everyone knew everyone else and you watched out for each other. It was like that on our dead end street, but not in the general community.

I want to mention two other distinct areas of Plainfield: the Netherwood area and Sleepy Hollow. Both were in the southern corner of the East End of Plainfield. Very few black folks lived in the handsome middle-class Netherwood neighborhoods. And I would bet absolutely none lived in the wealthy Sleepy Hollow neighborhood adorned with huge mansions.

So, there were distinct sectors in Plainfield, but no one was automatically, racially locked or restricted to one place. Many years later, I worked near Bayonne, New Jersey. Black and white friends who lived in Bayonne told me, unequivocally, that there were areas from which black folks knew they better stay away. I felt the same sort of neighborhood exclusivity in the Iron Bound section of Newark when I worked there for several years. But never in Plainfield. However, there was a financial barrier. You see, you could live anywhere in Plainfield you wanted—you just had to be able to afford it. And that barrier extended to poor white families as well.

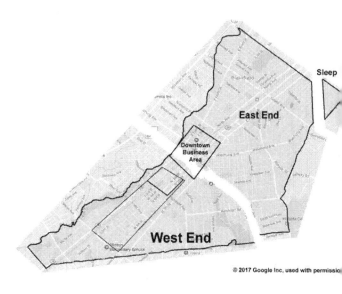

© 2017 Google Inc, used with permission

Nevertheless, in Plainfield in the early 1960s, I rode my bike all over the city, in and out of white neighborhoods all the time. No one ever said a word to me. No cop asked me where I was going or what I was doing. For the most part, everyone lived in harmony, everyone did their own thing; Plainfield as a city worked and it worked well. In many ways, it was a wonderful place to live.

From Thursday night to Saturday night, the downtown especially came alive. Remember, there were no malls as we have them today. The closest one, the Menlo Park Mall, was very small and thirteen miles away; it was nothing like the way it is now. You would hardly go there when there were a ton of good stores in your own city that had everything you wanted. Saturday was particularly fun in downtown Plainfield. Buck and Benny's Sporting Goods, Sears and Roebuck Department Store, the Acme and A&P grocery markets, Globe Shoes, Littman's Diamonds, Winters Bakery, The Beverly Hat Shop, The Surprise Store, Strand Movie Theatre, Tepper's Department Store, the Park Tearoom, Matthews Furniture Store, Van Arsdales's Shoes, Lazaar's Stationery, and Woolworths were just a few of the hundreds of prosperous businesses that truly came to life on Saturdays. There was at least one business in downtown Plainfield that was owned by a black family—Brook's Record store. If you wanted a Beethoven or Tchaikovsky long playing album you went to Gregory's Music Store, but if you wanted a small 45 recording of James Brown, Martha and the Vandellas, or Chubby Checker, you went to Brook's, and for about 50 cents, you owned some good music.

The difference between Gregory's Music Store and Brook's Record Store pretty much reflected the nature of the black and white Plainfields, at least from a black perspective. Both stores did well. Gregory's was bigger and had been around longer. Brook's was smaller and had soul music playing on the inside, and you were warmly greeted.

Gregory's opened its doors to everyone, but it felt a bit cold, while Brook's felt warm and cozy inside. Ironically, I preferred the classical music from Gregory's and spent a lot of money there. But I felt at home at Brooks.

Although well established and profitable, neither would survive for my son or grandson to see.

3 DIFFERENT VOICES

1965.

By the mid-sixties, our nation and my hometown of Plainfield were being affected by all the social changes that were happening at the time. An elegant and young president had been assassinated two years earlier. Plainfield, as a city, shut down on Monday, November 25, 1963, the day of President Kennedy's funeral. All schools were closed; it was a national day of mourning. I watched the television intently and sadly as the state funeral for President Kennedy played out. By noon, the cortege escorting his body reached a Catholic cathedral in Washington. Since much of the service was in Latin, I couldn't relate to those proceedings. So, I grabbed my three-year-old brother and we walked to the downtown of Plainfield.

I was surprised by what I saw.

And what I saw was no one.

The normally busy streets of our business district were absolutely silent. No people, no cars— no one. It was bizarre to see traffic lights continuously doing their green-yellow-red thing without one car anywhere nearby. Every store we passed by had a sign with a message similar to this:

OUR STORE IS CLOSED TODAY IN HONOR OF OUR LATE PRESIDENT

or

BECAUSE OF THE DEATH OF PRESIDENT KENNEDY WE WILL NOT BE OPEN TODAY

I had not seen anything like that before or since.

I remember television commentators saying something about that time that I didn't quite get at the moment. They spoke of America losing its innocence with the murder of its young president, and how we would never be the same. I now realize how true it was. The child-like wonder I had of many things including my home of Plainfield just didn't seem the same after those four horrible days.

That was 1963. By 1965, many things had truly changed.

Our president was no longer a young intellectual from Massachusetts; he was an older guy from Texas. And while President Kennedy made great speeches about civil rights, Lyndon Baines Johnson actually attacked the civil rights problems in the United States and started a "War on Poverty." During his first State of the Union Address, President Johnson announced his "Great Society" initiative. Later in that same year, Johnson quoted the theme of the civil rights movement to Congress when he emphatically said, *"We shall overcome!"* It was a stirring moment.

Technology had advanced a lot too.

The space program had moved from a single guy in a capsule to two guys in a Gemini orbiter. The Apollo moon ships, and the giant Saturn rockets to propel them, were soon to be on the assembly line. More TV shows filmed in color were being produced (although most Americans still had black-and-white TVs). While automakers were installing seat belts in their cars, many for the first time, 1965 marked the launch of Ford's uniquely-designed Mustang.

The "conflict" in Vietnam was being referred to more and more as a "war" as thousands of American combat troops were being sent there every month. At the same time, those against the war were massing and protesting in equally-growing numbers.

Our music had changed. Elvis Presley, Brenda Lee, and Bo Diddley were upstaged by The Beatles, The Rolling Stones, and other British groups. Many American singers were starting to use their music to protest the war and spotlight social injustice.

I was no longer a kid but a teenager in high school. My family had moved yet again to another home in the West End. With the help of school, television, and newspapers, I started to see the world beyond the pleasant, safe confines of Plainfield. And one issue was bothering me more and more—civil rights.

As American soldiers were being put in peril in far-off Southeast Asia, innocent American civilians were in danger right here in Mississippi and Alabama. Martin Luther King was at his apex of leadership as he mobilized courageous protestors to resist the racist, unconstitutional laws of the South. People were beaten and some were killed as they marched against the tyranny of segregation laws and culture. Almost every night on the TV news, we could see the battle for civil rights being played out on the screens. Those two events, the Vietnam War and the civil rights movement, in my opinion, ignited something here in America. Many blacks who remained quietly content during the late 50s and early 60s with "white American" culture were no longer beholden to that life style. The color blindness of that time was fading; the civil rights movement had installed new vision.

More and more blacks were rejecting what they had been fed for generations. On television, it suddenly became clear that the happy families from the *Donna Reed Show*, *Father Knows Best*, *Leave it to Beaver*, and dozens more were only white families. The heroes of all action shows and movies were white men. Even cartoon and comic book heroes were all white dudes. Oh, you might see a few black faces when it came to music or sports. But in the real world, when you saw black folks on television, they were usually being beaten, water-hosed, jailed, or murdered by cowardly southern cops and Ku Klux Klan members. Night after night, month after month, year after year— that constant presentation of horror was affecting people in profound many ways, including myself.

Just as many young white college students had had enough of the Vietnam War and were starting to protest it, many young black people were tired of seeing other innocent blacks wrongfully beaten, arrested, and suppressed. They could no longer live by the godly themes that Martin Luther King inspired in his courageous campaign against injustice. No, more and more black folks had had enough of the naked displays of racism in this country. The fury of witnessing so many wrongs and nothing being done about them had reached the boiling point. Inequality had gone on too long and they were not willing to wait any longer. They were going to do something about it.

And that something was the Watts riots of 1965.

I believe that event in Los Angeles, California lit a match on a long fuse that traveled three thousand miles and took two years to reach the East coast and, eventually, the city of Plainfield in 1967.

California had also experienced the "Great Migration" like the grand northern cities had over the decades of the early 20th century. And just like many of the northern cities, those blacks, because of lower education thus lower income, were relegated to specific areas within the large cities. Although laws in California didn't permit segregation in housing, many areas had housing that was too expensive for newcomers to the state. The economics of the situation caused many of the minorities to dwell in places that supported, at least in concept, low-income housing.

The historically white communities of Compton and Watts resisted the influx of blacks. South Los Angeles soon became the site of significant racial violence. Whites started to bomb and shoot at houses owned by blacks in those two cities. They even set burning crosses on the lawns of homes purchased by black families. White gangs in nearby cities such as Huntington Park and South Gate would attack blacks if they traveled in their areas.

Those racially-motivated events were building a time bomb of their own in the communities. As I watched the craziness of the Southern racist situation on television, so were the blacks from Compton and Watts. And while I was satisfied to allow the civil rights movement led by Dr. King to eventually find a way to justice, many other young blacks in the Los Angeles area were losing their patience. They looked around at their communities and saw unfair housing, lack of decent paying jobs, and racial bigotry. And those black Los Angeles communities had to deal with something I never experienced in Plainfield—a police force they felt was out to get them.

In the 1960s, the Los Angeles Police Department (LAPD) thought of themselves as a world-class police force. They considered themselves professional and disciplined. However, the black and Hispanic communities considered them unfair, racially prejudiced, and brutal. Many who lived in the area at the time, and observed such practices by the LAPD, point to their vicious behavior as one of the reasons why the Watts riots broke out on Wednesday, August 11, 1965.

The riot itself started over something relatively simple. A CHP (California Highway Patrol) officer stopped a young black man because the officer observed him driving recklessly in the Watts area of Los Angeles. The young person's mother and brother came to the arrest scene, where the mother chastised her son publicly for getting into trouble. Crowds slowly assembled around the scene. Soon, the mother was arguing with the police officers; some physical shuffling occurred between them. More cops arrived, and they decided to arrest all involved. The crowd, not sure what was going on, started spreading rumors of cops beating up old ladies and a pregnant woman. In time, angry mobs assembled and started throwing things at the cops.

More cops raced to the scene and tried to dismiss the crowd. But instead of breaking up and going home, the crowds grew in size and anger. Rocks, bricks, and concrete objects were being thrown at cops for much of the night.

The next day, black community leaders and the cops tried to calm things down. They sat down and discussed how to control the situation. But nothing was accomplished at the meeting.

Los Angeles police chief William H. Parker asked for help from the California National Guard. In my opinion, Chief Parker was delusional of what was going on. If you were not alive at the time, it would be hard for you to grasp all of the events that could affect someone's thinking and decision-making back then. The Vietnam War was in place; we were in a Cold War with the communists. Parker lived near Hollywood where fictional good and bad guys were created in films. Hollywood also created fictional ways of how to deal with supposed bad guys. Parker saw force as the only way to deal with "the bad guys." He publicly said that the police were dealing with "people acting like monkeys." In his mind, the riots appeared to be a rebellion against the government, and he was determined to put it down.

By Friday, August 13, the rioting grew worse. Thousands of soldiers from the National Guard and hundreds of cops attempted to restore order in Watts. But the looting spread, especially to white businesses in the area. Any white motorists who drove their cars into that area during the unrest were pulled out of their cars by angry rioters and beaten up. News reporters described the situation as being like a warzone. They didn't feel they were in the United States.

Law enforcement struck back. More than 15,000 cops and soldiers engaged the large riot zone that now covered miles. Police killed many rioters, which made the other rioters even more incensed. They burned hundreds of buildings and any police car they could find unguarded. Firefighters who tried to stop blazes were attacked by rioters. Police were arresting people by the thousands, and strict curfews in black areas were put in place. Before the riot ended on Sunday, August 15th, thirty-four people had been killed, all except three by the police.

Subsequent reports indicate that more than 30,000 people were involved one way or another during the six-day battle. More than a thousand were injured and well over $40 million worth of damage done.

I watched all of it on television, I heard it on the radio, I read about it in the newspapers, day after day during and long after the riot. I drew several conclusions of my own. First, the whole thing was an insult to President Johnson and Martin Luther King. Both, in their own ways, had tried hard to avoid such a clash here in America. It would now be difficult for President Johnson to go to Congress to seek more rights for "Negroes," as he (politely, for the time) put it, when the Negroes were trying to burn down a major American city. Until then, blacks were always the victims of hateful action. Dr. King implored for peace constantly. For him to see such massive violence and destruction, it must have wounded his heart in ways few would comprehend.

But I also understood the rioters. On the same TV screen in my house that displayed rioters in Los Angeles doing stupid things, I had seen white sheriffs, KKK members, and racist white citizens do absolutely horrible things to blacks down South. Now, the godly part of me felt Dr. King was courageously correct in his non-violent path. But the young person in me who had to deal with his own growing anger understood why the young blacks were demonstrating their rage. I saw innocent white motorists beaten in Watts; I saw innocent black kids beaten by cops in Mississippi. Both were wrong, both were hurtful to watch.

But something else upset me, even scared me, about that riot in Watts.

I didn't think it would end there.

I couldn't see that engine of anger being contained in California. Mainly because I didn't think the Californians had had it that bad. Oh, I'm sure they had legitimate complaints with their system. But it was nothing like the violent and suppressive systems of the South. So, to me, if the calm and cool people of Los Angeles would riot, my God, what would happen in other places?

And in many ways, I was correct. City riots like the one in Watts didn't take place down South. Dr. King's peaceful demonstrations and marches at least allowed people to vent. However, it was the blacks in Northern cities who were bottling up a furious resentment for the racism, bigotry, and prejudice that they saw in the media and faced themselves on a daily basis.

And that resentment, like a virulent infection, was about to spread.

4 TROUBLE COMES TO NEW JERSEY

I wanted to mention the Watts riots because, at the time, they were the biggest and most expensive in the cost of lives and property. But in truth, there had been an outbreak of race riots before and after Watts; they were just a lot smaller. However, they all had a terrible effect on their communities.

In 1964, there were racial disturbances in Rochester, New York City, Philadelphia, and Chicago. There were also problems in the New Jersey cities of Jersey City, Paterson, and Elizabeth.

In 1965, the Watts riots took center stage.

In 1966, there was unrest in Cleveland known as the Hough riots; there was also racial trouble in San Francisco and Cleveland and in Chicago again with the Division Street riots.

1967 was a horrific year for riots. There was the 12th Street riot in Detroit, the Harlem riot, the Cambridge riot in Maryland, and Rochester was hit again. Twelve other cities suffered from riots that year, including Newark—and Plainfield.

Although each of the events was a unique experience for the cities suffering from the hostilities, there was an unfortunate uniformity about the calamities: the violence almost always started in and centered on poorer sections of the city. Those sections were always overwhelmingly populated by minorities. All of the riots took place during the summer when schools were out and many young people were not employed and had nothing to do. And almost all were triggered by a small confrontation between a couple of police officers and a few blacks over a relatively minor thing that escalated to a contingent of police facing an angry crowd.

All of this was happening while Martin Luther King was down South pleading for non-violent ways of correcting racism. He could not be everywhere, and his message of peace was not being heard by overheated, underemployed young people up North.

******

The Newark riot was the largest act of civil disobedience New Jersey ever faced. It was one of the major and most destructive race riots in the nation. Started on July 12th, 1967, it had all the ingredients of previous riots: a large disenfranchised population of young blacks living in a city that was heavily populated by minorities, few of whom were in power. The white mayor, Hugh Addonizio, did little to avert the situation. Although the city was almost 50% black, few of the mayor's staff or people in power were of color. And although Newark was one of the first cities in America to hire black police officers, there were relatively few on the force. With all due respect to those black officers, they were just tokens. There were far too few of them to make any difference in the community. But on paper, the city could say they had minorities on the police force. In reality, you had white officers going into predominantly black neighborhoods, and those white officers were often accused by the black communities of stopping, questioning, and harassing young blacks with little or no reason.

You would have thought and hoped that Newark officials would have learned from the Watts riot and other violent episodes across the country that the mixture of white officers sent into predominantly black sectors to solve problems during the summer was a volatile mix. Yet, the mayor and his teams did little to prevent that dangerous formula.

And so it happened...

On July 12th, a black cab driver was arrested by white police officers in a heavily black sector of the city. Heated words were exchanged, and the cops beat up the cab driver. This was probably nothing new, except this time, it was witnessed by people living in a large public housing project known as the Hayes Homes. According to them, they saw a beaten and unconscious black man being taken into the local (4th Precinct) police headquarters. That part of the story was probably true. However, from that point on, rumors started and spread. And since rumors have a life of their own, the story of the incident grew in size and severity to the point that people believed that the cab driver had been killed by the cops and that they had taken the body inside the station to hide it. In truth, the cab driver was released with his lawyer shortly after being arrested. Keep in mind there were no cell phones and social media back then. There was no way to share up-to-the-minute accurate information. So, the false information of the rumors continued as truth.

On that hot summer evening, hot upset people—who held onto visions of black folks being abused by Southern cops, murdered by racist organizations, and killed in recent riots—finally had enough. Angry crowds went to that police station located deep in the black Central Ward. White police officers ran out to confront the mob. The crowd started throwing bottles, bricks, and rocks at the cops. When the police were reinforced, the crowds left and went to City Hall, where they shouted and ranted about their displeasure with the situation. With night setting in, looters started smashing windows of stores and throwing merchandise into the streets. Liquor stores, and there were a lot of them in Newark, were hit especially hard. False fire alarms had engine companies racing around the city, while looters hit places with little protection.

The next evening, rioters attacked a different police station, the 5th Precinct building, with rocks, bottles, and other missiles. The police responded in force with clubs. Looting began along the busy and vital Springfield Avenue. It was no longer the small businesses in hidden corners of the city being looted; no, the violence had blatantly graduated to being done right out in the open and on a main street. Cars were set on fire, responding police were being struck by bricks. Back in those days, there were no real SWAT teams. Officers had their six-shot revolvers and not much more. When things got out of control, ordinary cops with no special training were issued larger weapons and told what to do as the situation flexed. So after the brick attack on the 5th Precinct and the downtown looting, some of the cops were given shotguns and the entire force was placed on emergency duty. Before the sun came up, the situation had gotten so bad that the New Jersey National Guard was called in to reinforce the police.

By the third evening, it was essentially warfare in Newark. It reached that level after an innocent woman, Rebecca Brown, who was doing nothing, was killed by a hail of bullets wrongly directed at her second floor apartment window.

That event exploded the situation.

For the next few days rioting, shooting, looting, burning, and direct confrontation between blacks and law enforcement cost the lives of 16 innocent civilians, 8 suspected looters, 1 police officer, and 1 firefighter. In addition, almost 700 people, including police and military personnel, were injured. More than 1,400 were arrested and millions of dollars of damage done.

For the perpetually peaceful, prosperous town of Plainfield, the Newark riot was like a large virus that could not be contained. With the help of television, an existing bad condition, and outside agitators, the corruption of that virus was to spread and contaminate my hometown.

And it made us all very sick.

5 "I HAVE A BAD FEELING ABOUT THIS."

I love television, I always have. I had asthma as a kid. With few if any effective medicines available at that time, if I incurred an asthma attack, it meant four miserable days in bed for me. The preventative was no running, no sports, and staying in the house during hot humid days. Television, radio, and the newspapers became my eyes and ears to the outside, and I gorged on information from those sources. But there was another vehicle for local news—the grapevine. People telling another person a story and then having it passed on again was an art form back then. Of course, the method was susceptible to being highly inaccurate; however, it was rather dramatic and great fun. Few things were better than telling a friend a hot news item. My mother was especially good at receiving and spreading gossip. With six kids and a husband to tend to, she only left the house on Saturday afternoons to shop for groceries and on Sundays for church. Her connection to the hot, local gossip came through the telephone. I retain vivid imagery of Mom, phone handle to ear, and the long phone cord tethered to the wall. Once dinner dishes were cleaned up, Mom would get on the phone in the kitchen from 6:30 to 8:30 with her friends. They would exchange all sorts of juicy news. If I were to walk by her, I would hear things like:

"No, she didn't!"
"Lord, have mercy."
"Hmm, hmm, hmm."
"He did what?!"
"That's what she told me..."

All of that and more were mixed with dramatic pauses and a lot of laughter. Mom did not restrict my TV watching, my radio listening, or my newspaper reading. So, I couldn't have cared less if she spent all evening on the phone; it made her happy. However, I learned early on that the news could be frightening when things got dark in the world.

The first time media news frightened me was during the Cuban Missile Crisis. At the height of that crazy event, the TV and newspapers were predicting that we were close to nuclear war with the Russians. I was eleven years old in 1962 when those events happened, and it scared the hell out of me.

I was twelve years old and traumatized again in November 1963 when all my news sources reported the assassination of President Kennedy.

In February 1965, I was fourteen and emotionally better-prepared for the assassination of Malcolm X.

By 1967, I was sixteen and in high school. I was studying about body counts in Vietnam, the murders of civil rights workers, little girls blown up at church, and the burning and looting of American cities.

When I read of the Newark riots, when I saw the violent pictures on the TV news, I was shaken just a bit. Up until then, almost all of the major tragedies in the news happened somewhere else. As awful as Vietnam was, the fighting was 8,500 miles away. The racial craziness with the dogs, water hoses, and beatings were way down South.

But the Newark riot was just a few miles away. I had been to Newark; the whole thing concerned me.

However, I still felt that Plainfield was immune to such things. Actually, trouble in Plainfield was the furthest thing from my mind in 1967. I had gotten my first job. Plainfield had set aside some money to employ teenagers during the summer in various temporary jobs. I was fortunate to get one of those jobs. Positions included helping school janitors with their summer cleaning and repairs of their buildings. Other temporary jobs were with the Public Works Department, which cleaned and repaired city streets and parks. I was assigned to work at one of the city's playgrounds. As a junior counselor, I got to teach kids how to play games and have fun from 9 a.m. to 4 p.m. Monday to Friday at Rushmore Playground deep in the West End of Plainfield. I was paid $1.40 per hour, which for a teenager was pretty good at the time. I believe my two supervisors worked as teachers during the winter and were senior counselors at the playground during the summer. One of them, a Mr. Crowley, would pick me up for work, and he would often drive me back home after we closed the playground. He was a decent and fair man, but what I remember most about him—he had a new Corvette. Up until then, the coolest car I had ever been in was a rusty Ford station wagon, our family car. Zipping along with him in that red rocket was a treat.

So with the school year done, world and national news far away, and my everyday world occupied with a pleasant job, I thought the summer of 1967 would be enjoyable and profitable.

But something started to happen in Plainfield.

Now, this part of my story is hard to quantify or describe accurately, but it's an important part of the picture—I think you'll get my point. When you live in a house, or a town, or go to a school, or have a job in the same place for a long time, you gain a feeling for the environment surrounding those things. You can just feel when everything is OK, but equally importantly, you can detect when something is wrong.

You get into your car, something you've done hundreds of times, but this time, something feels out of place.

A parent or a child can just look at each other and detect if something is wrong.

Well, I felt that something was wrong about Plainfield as we approached mid-July of 1967. To be a bit more precise, I detected that something didn't feel right about the West End of the city. But before I go into that a bit more, let me give you a quick snapshot of Plainfield just before the riot.

The downtown of Plainfield was thriving. The big annual art show was days away.

The event first started in 1963 and had become a big favorite of the summer. All the streets of downtown Plainfield were turned into showplaces for all sorts of art. Tables and easels were lined up and down all the streets, in front of every store, near every corner. Hundreds of artists exhibited more than 3,000 paintings, photographs, and sculptures in downtown Plainfield. All of the businesses loved the art show; it brought thousands of extra people to the shopping areas (especially people with money). The artists themselves competed for big prize awards. All of this was sponsored by the Central Jersey Chamber of Commerce, also located in Plainfield. No one knew it at the time, but the art festival of 1967 very well might have been the high point of those "Queen City" days in Plainfield. Ironically, just a few hours before the start of the race riot, thousands of white folks were roaming the streets of downtown Plainfield with a complete sense of security, pouring money into the businesses and city coffers.

I was aware of the art festival and all the buzz and excitement that it created. But I was also aware that something just didn't feel right about the West End. It was just about mid-July; the normally high summer temperatures were pretty moderate. Nevertheless, in those days, at least in black West End sections, few people, if any, had air conditioning. Relief from the heat came from electric fans—or you went outside, particularly in the evening. Late in the day, you would find middle-aged and older black folks sitting on their front porch—it was an old tradition that went back a hundred years. Some racist white folks of that era often labeled black folks as "porch monkeys." This was in spite of the fact that porch sitting used to be seen as a sign of wealth among white folks long ago. Nevertheless, in 1967, porch sitting meant it was too warm in the house, or there was nothing to watch on television (TV was limited to less than ten channels back then). If you would walk or ride your bike through black communities, as I often did, you would see a lot of that porch sitting.

As I biked through the neighborhoods during mid-July, I noticed older black teens and guys in the their early 20s hanging around porches and street corners, doing nothing. That was not unusual; there just seemed to be more of them. And some of them I had never seen before. I didn't hear them say anything particularly poisonous or alarming. But there was an unfriendly vibe about them. I believe that resentment was a reaction to current events.

Wednesday, July 12th, 1967 was the first day of the Newark riot.

Television and newspapers had started reporting on the disturbance. Although the worst days were ahead, there were enough rumors and grapevine chat to set people off. Many Plainfielders had friends and relatives in Newark. There was no doubt that back channel information from them was finding its way to the West End neighborhoods, porches, and street corners. So those unfamiliar people I had seen, mixed with local troublemakers, were aware of and perhaps becoming inflamed by the Newark riot stories.

So the scenario in the West End of Plainfield was slowly starting to match the patterns that had thrown other urban cities across the country into racial chaos. Parts of the formula: a summer month; and large pockets of relatively young disenfranchised blacks, who were underemployed and not included in the city power structure, were at hand. The other parts of the formula: those young blacks becoming angry over an event, and—the final piece of the recipe—a confrontation with white police officers, which could happen at any time.

I detected that budding energy during that mid-July week.

Now, did I think that a riot was coming to Plainfield? No, absolutely not. I don't think the mayor, police, city council members, or anyone else in authority detected problems coming our way. But there was no doubt in my mind that the atmosphere in the West End of Plainfield was hostile.

But, hey, the art festival was three days away.

Most Plainfielders were focusing on that.

6 "TROUBLE STARTS IN PLAINFIELD"

Friday, July 14th, 1967 started off as a bad day in Newark.

Civil unrest in New Jersey's largest city had been going on for two days. By Friday, officials in Newark felt the situation was getting out of hand. Police were given more weapons and told to "fire if necessary." The New Jersey State Police and the New Jersey National Guard were also called in to help stabilize a worsening situation. Governor Richard Hughes, describing the situation in Newark as "a city in open rebellion," decided to set up a command post in Newark. He wanted to be near to help Mayor Addonizio regain control of the situation. Legal steps were being prepared to install curfews, close all liquor stores, and to shut down sporting goods stores to stop the distribution of weapons.

Meanwhile, in Plainfield, Friday morning started off as another calm summer day.

In the last chapter, I told you that I felt something different about the West End of Plainfield where the majority of blacks lived. But it was just a feeling. In my opinion, based upon living my whole life in the town, I doubted that Plainfielders would have initiated a violent confrontation in the city.

Friday afternoon, still no problem in Plainfield. But a little bit of city culture was going to be a factor in the trouble to come.

Although McDonalds and other fast food places had already started in the United States, they were still in relative infancy in 1967. There were no franchised fast food places in Plainfield at that time. But there were hungry teenagers, and they sought out the places that cost the least and tasted the best. The Texas Weiner on Watchung Avenue, the Red Tower on Park Avenue, and the White Star Diner on West Front Street were three of the most popular sources of fast food (and amazingly, all three are still in business today).

As a rule, our family never went out to eat; we just couldn't afford it. My dad was a self-employed carpenter. However, if he asked me to work with him on a weekend, it also meant I had the treat of breakfast at a diner. Those early morning meals at the White Star Diner were the only times I had been in there. Friends boasted that they served great tasting hamburgers. And I might have tried to go there and get one on my own, but White Star was located in an area that my mother suggested I stay away from.

Understanding the unofficial sectors of Plainfield is very important from this point on.

If the Plainfield police had to protect three areas of the city with all their might, in my opinion, first and foremost would have been the business district. The second and third places to protect would be Muhlenberg Hospital district and, finally, Sleepy Hollow and the wealthier areas of the Netherwood neighborhood. Now, every place in Plainfield would get a police response, but it varied by area. As an adult, years later, I requested and got permission from the Plainfield Police Department to go along with them as a "ride along" in their city patrols. I sat in the back seat of the police car as they patrolled the neighborhoods. It was fascinating to observe how the police handled every sort of situation from attempted break-ins of private homes to bar fights. I also noted how they unevenly handled problems on the predominantly white East End of town as compared to the "blacker" West End.

The White Star Diner was located in a place to which the police might or might not respond quickly or comprehensively when called for help.

* * * * * *

Friday night, July 14th.

The White Star Diner, located deep in the black community, was having a busy evening. Although very popular, the diner was relatively small. So, if you stopped by for a burger and saw the place packed, you might just hang around and wait for someone to leave. Well, on that Friday night, the place was overflowing with young customers. Many more waited outside the place. Something I've learned about young people long ago: one-on-one, almost all teenagers are interesting. Even the worst of them will display some thought and individuality. However, put a couple of them together and they can get a bit silly. Assemble more than a dozen of even the smartest teens and before long, they'll all be laughing at the stupidest of things. Individual responsibility will be tossed out. Gather more than thirty teens, unsupervised, in one location, and a sort of groupthink takes over. Well, by eleven o'clock on that hot Friday night, a crowd of more than 150 teenage boys and girls, mostly black, were in and outside the White Star Diner.

I would be nervous around 150 Harvard University freshmen unsupervised at night.

So, with a large number of young people assembled around the White Star Diner, silliness and childishness were certain to be on the menu.

Soon, they were no longer interested in food; they got louder and more rambunctious. If the police were called, they did not respond. By some accounts, one police car did drive by rather quickly without stopping. I'm going to assume the cops drove by to observe the situation and report what they saw to higher-ups.

I'm sure there are many versions of what happened next that changed the more-or-less lighthearted situation around the diner to a hostile one. No single story has total confirmation, but a large number of young people who were there stated that at around 11 p.m., four or five young white guys, who appeared out of nowhere, tossed a bottle filled with gasoline at a passing car near the diner. The bottle did not explode, but it broke and the flying glass allegedly cut some of the black youth. Word spread of the incident, and that single action, according to many, was the spark that turned the crowd from teens having a good time on a Friday night to a mob. At any rate, those white boys left the scene immediately.

As the horde was going through a metamorphosis, those who came for a hamburger or some late night fun with a date left or separated from the crowd. Those who wanted to cause a little commotion or do some venting stayed. But as the transmutation was completed and aggression became the theme, the majority of the young people dispersed. About 40 remained and they started looking for trouble.

It could be said that the Plainfield riot started at that moment.

That group of 40 left the diner and started moving east on West Front Street in the general direction of the main business district. Along the way, they shouted various things as they marched along the sidewalk and street, with each step becoming more belligerent. Still, at the moment, they were not much more than a very noisy crowd. As it approached midnight, they were certainly heard by peaceful families in their homes as they continued to leap and yell along Front Street. It's most likely that some of those peaceful family members reported the aberrant behavior to the police. But the police did not respond.

The crowd of 40 arrived at Plainfield Avenue. Instead of going further toward the business district, they turned right onto Plainfield Avenue and headed south.

They walked a block or so past the large Elmwood Gardens housing project that was on their left. That 120-unit, low-income dwelling, which extended from Plainfield Avenue east to Elmwood Place, was simply known as "The Projects." The large, multi-story apartment compound was built in 1961 and therefore relatively new. But it always seemed to be a magnet for trouble. The impromptu assembly continued on Plainfield Avenue, past Second Street, to Third Street. They collected themselves there on Plainfield Avenue between Third and Fourth Streets at two other well-known locations in the black community: the Plainfield Avenue Playground (now known as Hannah Atkins Playground) and the West End Gardens (now known as the Joanne Hollis Gardens). The West End Gardens were another low-income, 128-unit apartment complex. For the next week, that location was considered by the police to be the unofficial home base of the rioters.

It's interesting to note that those two low-income housing projects were probably an effort by the city to help the black community in some way when they were built in 1961 and 1954. But in Plainfield, and in many other cities where constructions like the Elmwood Gardens were created, they turned into hives of corruption and despair. And many were destined to be torn down, as Elmwood Gardens was, because they had become major crime centers.

The mob of 40 nested near the West End Gardens for a while. They were loud and threatening, and they occasionally threw objects at passing cars. Still, the police did not intervene.

Now, past midnight, the mob went on the move again. They backtracked along Plainfield Avenue to West Second Street. They turned right and headed east toward the center of town. It was that potential threat to all those businesses, just hours before the big art festival, that brought out the authorities. By the time the mob reached Madison Avenue and West Second Street, they were met by a large contingent of Plainfield police. Now, the 40-person mob was not really organized. They didn't have a viable agenda; they were after hamburgers a few hours earlier. Nevertheless, they ran around an empty parking lot; some of them threw things at a few stores. But after a while, they turned around and headed west on West Second Street. It was after 1 a.m. by then. They threw objects at any passing car, especially if white folks were in the car. On the way back to Plainfield Avenue, they smashed a few store windows and car windshields. There were a couple of fistfights, and they allegedly threw a Molotov cocktail at a police car that fortunately did not ignite.

Once the alarm was sounded that a mob of blacks were "terrorizing" the neighborhood, three brave adult black men inserted themselves into the heart of the throng when they returned to the West End Gardens. Councilman Everett C. Lattimore, his brother George Lattimore, and businessman Harvey L. Judkins, who was also on the city council, did their best to de-escalate the situation very early that Saturday morning. They questioned the young people to find out why they were doing what they were doing. They stayed and listened to them for hours. By 4 a.m., everyone grew weary enough to go home without further incident.

Reporters from the Courier News spoke to the three peacemakers while still on the scene. Councilman Lattimore reported that the young people were boiling over with frustration. They shouted concerns that ranged from police brutality to the lack of a community swimming pool. They even went so far as to voice concerns as to why the federal government was wasting time and money on Vietnam instead of dealing with school busing and more low-income housing here in America. Now, how all of this surfaced from a visit to a hamburger joint is something of a mystery. However, some of the individuals admitted that their behavior was prompted by what was happening in Newark and they were reflecting the concerns of black folks there.

That made more sense that trying to link Vietnam to fries and a Coke.

Newspapers were really serious and fast about their work back in those days. A report of the early Saturday-morning violence, including the short interview with the three adult community leaders, and even an interview with the mayor of Plainfield, was in the Saturday edition of the paper and out for distribution on the same day.

From those newspaper reports, it was interesting to note that the white mayor of

Plainfield, George Hetfield, described the Friday/Saturday incidents as "youthful lawlessness." And although comments from councilman Lattimore clearly pointed to social frustrations as part of the energy behind the disturbance, the mayor refused to consider any deep-seated racial issues as a possible source of the problem.

Ironically, the white mayor of Newark, Hugh Addonizio, was essentially saying the same thing about problems in his city, and so was the white governor at the time. So, it was white men, in high places, with no direct contact with the black youths of their cities, who had decided that the disturbances had little to do with a long-term social situation. They were simply cases of "lawlessness."

To me, that lack of understanding, the lack of contact, the blindness as to what was happening across America, were just as much part of the problem as anything else. Let me be clear: I cannot and will not justify violence of any type. But I do understand how violence happens when two conflicting sides are completely out of communication with one another.

Everett Lattimore, George Lattimore, and Harvey Judkins were not blind. Those good leaders were keenly aware of the urban warfare going on 18 miles away in Newark. They were also aware of the history of the last few years of the volatile civil rights movement in our country. And perhaps they detected the same unstable vibe I had when they visited their communities on the West End. They were in position to do something I couldn't at the time—to courageously try to stop a tragedy from happening in Plainfield.

7 "SMOLDERING"
SATURDAY, JULY 15TH

If the violence of Friday night/early Saturday morning had been associated with a fight after a high school football game, or after a rock concert, and with no racial overtones, the situation would have been contained, over and done with. However, the actions of last night were not just "lawlessness" as the mayor's oversimplified analysis proclaimed it. If Plainfield had no hidden racial problems, if the teens were after a hamburger on a cold December night with Christmas specials on TV rather than a race war in Newark, Friday night's circus of stupidity would not have even happened.

Unfortunately, those were not the conditions when people woke up bright and early on Saturday, July 15th, 1967 in Plainfield and learned what had happened overnight. Oh, I know there was hope, even confidence that the events of Friday night and early Saturday morning were over. But nobody knew for sure. Oh, and just to be accurate, the day did not start brightly, as it had rained early and there was a threat of rain all day long.

As I mentioned before, my family lived in the West End at the time. Our single-family home was on West Fourth Street right by the neighboring city of Piscataway. Actually, our backyard was in Piscataway. It was an awkward sight when it snowed to see a snow plow from Plainfield come right to our house and then turn around and go back toward Plainfield. Then a truck from Piscataway would come to our house and then turn around and go back. So, we were as west in Plainfield as could go.

Our Saturday started peacefully and routinely. The eight of us got up at various times and started our day, which included watching cartoons, making breakfast, washing clothes, and maybe cutting grass, if the weather held. I'm sure Mom's early morning phone calls from friends who lived in The Projects and West End Gardens had given her numerous accounts of what they had witnessed overnight. But none of that grapevine information was alarming enough to keep us away from our weekly trek to downtown Plainfield where we did all of our shopping.

I joined the family as we got into our old

station wagon and headed east along West Fourth Street. As we arrived at Plainfield Avenue, I didn't notice anything out of place. However, it seemed like there were more people just hanging around than normal.

Once we arrived in downtown Plainfield, there were absolutely no traces of any sort of problem. On the contrary, the big annual art festival was under way. Even with the constant threat of rain, hundreds of artists and thousands of pieces of art were displayed everywhere throughout the business district. The streets hummed with music and activity, clowns and performers roamed about entertaining the crowds of people. The lively celebration of art and culture made the trouble of last night seem like it had happened long ago and far away.

As Mom and Dad did their shopping, my siblings and I roamed around downtown never thinking for a moment that we were in any danger—and we were not. Everyone was calm, civilized, and happy. Yes, there was definitely a large police presence, but they were just in the background. Everything felt just fine.

******

Saturday evening.

Every Saturday was a big shopping day in downtown Plainfield. However, the art festival had doubled the bustle of the city. Nevertheless, it was still Saturday, and traditionally in Plainfield, everything began to shut down around 6 p.m. By 7 or 8 p.m., downtown Plainfield was very quiet. And that tranquility was usually the norm throughout the city.

Unfortunately, the rancor of the Friday night disturbance, although unseen and dormant while the sun was out, had returned that Saturday night. During the day, while large, peaceful, mainly white crowds were enjoying and supporting the arts, less than a mile away, there were many angry black folks in the West End cultivating dissension and planning trouble. Using telephones, the grapevine, and the rumor mill, those forty individuals from the night before had secured many more recruits. When the sun went down on that cloudy Saturday, trouble started near the West End Gardens on Plainfield Avenue and spread rapidly.

Reports started coming into Plainfield Police Headquarters of rocks being thrown at cars and fires started in trashcans and cars. When firefighters responded to the fires, individuals threw Molotov cocktails at them. Windows were smashed at several small stores which were then looted. As the night wore on, things got worse. If you were a white person on a bike or on foot, you were going to be, at the very least, harassed. If you were in a car, objects would be thrown at your vehicle. If you stopped at a traffic light, you might be pulled out of the car, beaten, and robbed. As the night wore on, if you were white, you might even be shot at.

When the local police deal with crime, even something on the level of a bank robbery, they don't normally notify the mayor or anyone of the senior municipal staff. But that Saturday night situation was different and was spreading; the chief of police, Milford Payne, notified city officials including the mayor. Soon, the situation was being monitored by the highest levels of the Plainfield government. It became evident to them that they, the people in authority, were being overwhelmed. So, they initiated two strategies. First, they identified the troubled area. Their tracking of events concluded that there was a 14-block area in the heart of the West End black community that was slipping into chaos. That area was outlined as Madison Avenue to the east, Plainfield Avenue to the west, West Front Street to the north and West Fifth Street to the south. That was the 14-block hot spot. Plainfield Avenue was an important road. It started at West Front Street and extended all the way through South Plainfield into Middlesex County. Many white folks drove along that road to get to downtown Plainfield. But on that evening, their cars would be targets of the rioters.

The next concern and need for strategy—do you go into that hot spot and stop events one-by-one, or do you just contain it? As Plainfield's leaders pondered that, they made an important decision without much delay—to call for help.

Plainfield was the largest city in the central Jersey area at the time. At some point, long before the riots, all of the municipalities surrounding Plainfield met and created what I would describe as a mutual defense pact. Essentially, if any town in that pact experienced a situation that would overwhelm their law enforcement abilities, they would put out a call for help. The other members of the pact would send units of their police force to the aid of the distressed police department. The results: the city in trouble would have access to dozens or even hundreds of extra officers, based upon the need of the situation. Similar agreements were made concerning the fire departments. On that Saturday night, when the Plainfield Police Department realized they were getting more calls than they could handle, they sounded the alarm and police from those smaller cities responded quickly. The initial plan—ask those extra police to watch the peaceful parts of Plainfield and do the standard patrols. That would allow the Plainfield Police to muster enough officers to go into that 14-block area and settle things down.

So, that strategy and tactics were initiated. The Plainfield Police started dissolving crowds and arresting offenders. They were making some headway when they got a big assist from an unexpected source—Mother Nature. A heavy rain descended upon the city. More than anything else, that helped to disperse the troublemakers and bring a tepid peace back to the area. However, many of those agitated individuals returned home to watch televised reports from Newark showing even more violence and a rising death toll.

8 "INSIDE PEACE MAKERS OUTSIDE AGITATORS"
July 16th

Sunday morning.

Our family attended church every Sunday morning, especially my mother. Our place of worship, Mount Zion AME Church, was inside that 14-block trouble zone and right next to Shiloh Baptist Church; so were Mount Olive Baptist Church and Faith Congregational Church. Just outside of that "hot spot" were at least four more black churches, three white churches, and one very prominent Jewish temple. The temple would not have services on Sunday, but that would be normal for them. However, the black and white churches should have been in operation. However, it was one of the few times my mother decided not to go; and if she didn't go, none of us did.

The flood of rumors and grapevine information was rampant. It would have been helpful to have gotten some official information on that Sunday morning as to what was happening in Plainfield. However, there was no source of official news. The reliable supplier of news in to the city was the Courier News; however, back then, they did not produce a Sunday edition of the paper. So, on the aftermath of a difficult night for Plainfield, many of the residents were clueless as to what actually happened.

Let me share with you what I think the difference is between the grapevine and rumors/gossip. For us, back then, the grapevine consisted mainly of trusted neighbors and friends sharing pretty reliable information. Again, without the Internet or any rapid social media, the grapevine was treasured. Rumors and gossip, on the other hand, were often lies, distortions, and speculations. Here's an example of the two.

1. On September 11, 2001, as the tragedies in New York unfolded, two friends of mine, who were in one of the World Trade Center buildings, explained how they escaped death on that day. I shared those first-hand accounts with others.

   To me, that was good grapevine info.

2. During the same 9/11 event, there were early reports that the planes that crashed

into the New York buildings had poisonous gas in them, and other reports that the Sears Tower in Chicago (now the Willis Tower) had been hit and planes were also slamming into the Golden Gate Bridge in San Francisco.

Those were pure rumors that obviously turned out to be false.

So, on that Sunday morning in Plainfield after a night of craziness, the grapevine *and* rumors were in control.

My mother had a lot of friends in the troubled area. Two of them were excellent sources of information, Mrs. Brunner and Mrs. Blair, who I believe were sisters. They were absolutely charming church-going ladies; I would guess both were in their late fifties or early sixties and both were widows, so they lived in a small apartment together. Mrs. Blair was a little bit more in charge of things; she was the one who would drive and plan their outings. Mrs. Brunner was a small person who reminded me of a pleasant Siamese cat. When she spoke, she would often close one of her eyes. That peculiar action, along with her gentle whisper of a voice, made her delivery compelling. When they came over for Christmas or just a visit, Mrs. Blair would always go into the kitchen to chat with Mom. But Mrs. Brunner would often spend time with my brothers and sisters reciting the most fascinating stories. I remember one story of how she witnessed, as a child herself, black people being beaten and terribly abused by whites down South. Her one-eyed delivery of the tragic tale held all of us spellbound. Her stories didn't make you angry as much they would make you sad. Well, when the sisters called our home on that Sunday morning and told of witnessing young people running wild, shooting guns, and setting fires, that made the whole thing real to me. And for the first time, I was a bit nervous.

Down the street, to the east of our home, just two small blocks away was Clinton Avenue. That street ran perpendicular to our West Fourth Street. On the corner of Clinton and Fourth was Clinton Elementary School. Not only was it a school, it represented the city; it was the most western outpost of Plainfield's government. If you turned left on Clinton and headed north for a couple blocks you would reach West Third street, then South Second Street. That area had several businesses: a small grocery store, a hardware store, and something like a Dairy Queen. The *rumor* was that those stores had had some trouble last night. They were black businesses, and were more than a mile from the hot zone; nevertheless, supposedly, the trouble had come that close to our home. More than just stores, the people who ran the businesses were familiar to us; we knew them by name, they knew us by sight. Little mom-and-pop businesses like that were totally linked to their communities. That's why I was surprised to hear rumors that anyone had done anything to those places.

In spite of everything that appeared to have happened, I still I could not accept that Plainfielders would seriously want to hurt other Plainfielders. And I was not the only one who felt that way.

On that same Sunday, there were enough people who really wanted the trouble to stop. A quick rally was set up to meet in Greenbrook Park, one of two large parks in Plainfield. Greenbrook Park was on the West End, ironically, just around the corner from the White Star Diner. Concerned civic leaders, and just ordinary citizens, wanted an opportunity to speak to people like Councilman Lattimore and Councilman Judkins. It was felt that if a dialogue could be kept open, that could prevent continuance or escalation of the hostilities.

So, a large number of good-intentioned people met at the park.

However...

Although Greenbrook Park is in Plainfield, it's not owned or policed by the city. Union County retained ownership of the park and their police force was in control of it. That caused a problem. As much as I think the mayor and top police authorities were out of touch with the black community, they were at least Plainfielders. I don't think they would have stopped that peaceful meeting in the park. On the contrary, I think they would have welcomed any calming voices. The Union County authorities had no such affinities with Plainfielders. They were an "outside" police force and practically all white. They were interested in protecting property and maintaining rules. In their limited thinking, permits had to be issued for any large gathering in the park. Common sense—it's Sunday, no county business offices were open to secure a permit—was not to be found. Plainfield was in a dangerous moment. There had been two nights of unrest, and if there was a chance to allow peacemakers, community leaders, and ministers to speak to the people and establish peace, you would have thought one brave, level-headed commander of the park police would have said—*let them do it!*

But in what I consider a stupid move, the Union County Park Police called the meeting unlawful and insisted that the crowd disperse. A small army of Union County Park Police escorted the crowd out of the park.

Now, let's stop for a moment and take a snapshot of what just happened.

Many black folks who lived in the West End of Plainfield used that park all the time. My mother constantly brought us, as small children, to Greenbrook to play on the swings and sand boxes. While there, I would see people riding their bikes and playing baseball, football, and basketball. Families would have picnics, seniors would play croquette; I would even see young men washing and waxing their cars in the park. I would bet that few, if any, of those users knew of Union County jurisdiction. So, when members of the neighborhood desperately needed a familiar place in their hometown to meet for an important cause, they were confronted by outside white police officers who would not allow them to listen to community leaders during a time of crisis.

In my opinion, any remaining hope to peacefully stop the violence ended with that thoughtless, tactless act.

So, the frustrated and angry members of that assemblage, who came to the park with a small hope of peace, returned to the hot zone angrier and full of resentment.

******

Outside agitators.

For those of you who did not experience the civil rights protests and the city riots, there was a controversial theory connected to those events. There were many who felt that much of the trouble was caused by outside agitators, troublemakers, and even criminals from far-off places who would come to a city going through problems and exacerbate those problems already in play. Then there were those who did not believe that theory at all, feeling that all of the trouble was homegrown. I had heard the concept of "outside agitators" argued on the TV news, in newspapers, and on the radio for years. But I had no way to determine if it was true or not.

However...

If there is one thing that I can add, unequivocally, to the history of that time, and specifically to the history of the Plainfield riots, it is that the theory of outside agitators is TRUE. At least, it was true in Plainfield. How do I know that it's true? Because I saw them with my own eyes!

Sunday afternoons were always kind of quiet at our home. After coming back home from church, and settling down, oh, around 2 p.m., Mom would start preparing dinner. Dad was usually in the garage building or fixing something. I was most likely in front of a TV set. My younger brothers and sisters were either playing with our cats, playing games, or playing outside. We were encouraged not to visit other people or to have visitors on Sunday afternoon. It wasn't meant to be mean, it was just an extension of the reverence of that day.

On that Sunday, of course, the news was about the troubles in Plainfield. We had not gone to church, so our input of news was limited. Now, one of the ways to receive and transmit gossip or grapevine news was going outside and sitting on the porch. You'd just sit there and if someone came by that you knew, you'd share what was going on. Friends on bikes were particularly good dispatchers of the latest news. So instead of my normal intake of Sunday afternoon movies, I decided to sit on the porch for a while.

As I mentioned before, we lived on West Fourth Street right on the Piscataway border. That section of West Fourth was neither busy nor quiet. You couldn't play a street game on it, as you'd be interrupted every few moments. But there wasn't a constant flow of traffic either. Nevertheless, West Fourth Street extended westerly to a main artery in the area—Washington Avenue in Dunellen. Washington Avenue could take you to Interstate 287, which connected to the NJ Turnpike, which connected to Route 95, which went up and down the entire East Coast. Now, our relatively quiet West Fourth Street was not the primary thoroughfare into Plainfield, but it could be, especially if you wanted to stay off the radar.

On that afternoon, while sitting on the steps, I observed the normal one or two cars per five minutes; then all of a sudden, I heard a lot of cars in the distance. Almost like a parade, a train of cars coming from the west approached our home. They stood out and caught my attention because everything about them was so odd. There was no GPS back then, so many times if one person knew where they were going and the others didn't, you would simply follow the car in front of you. That pattern of one car following another was pretty easy to spot back then. Well, these cars were definitely following each other. They were all driving slowly, as if observing the area, or letting people in neighborhood know they were there. They were all big four-door passenger sedans and all of them were overloaded with people. It was July and hot; all of the cars had their windows open, so you could see inside. Each of the cars had at least six people in them, all of them appeared to be young black men, and they didn't look happy.

It was my guess that they were not headed to a family reunion.

Many wore dark sunglasses, many had rags tied around their heads. Of course, I didn't know what was in the trunks of those cars. But whatever was in them, combined with the weight of the passengers, caused the back of the cars to drag very low, almost touching the street. Everything I had seen was suspicious, but did not verify outside agitators. However, there was one other thing I automatically looked for as a teen—and that told the story. I had a habit of looking at license plates when any car drove by. I think it was left over from a game I used to play in the car with my brothers as our family traveled: we would spot and name license plates. Well, with years of doing that for fun, it was just natural for me to glance at the plates of a car. Every last one of the plates of the twelve to fifteen cars that drove by my house was from out of state. Virginia, Georgia, Tennessee, they were all from Southern states, and not one of them was from New Jersey.

Outside agitators.

Suddenly, that term became extremely real to me. I had a mixed reaction after witnessing that sober motorcade. First, I had some really good juicy information to pass along the grapevine. But even more impactful, I just knew those guys were up to no good. I hate to be prejudicial; but I wasn't blind, and I wasn't stupid. I could almost feel the hate oozing out of those cars. There was no doubt in my mind they were seeking some opportunity to do something bad. I also felt someone had asked them to come to Plainfield.

Although our disturbances were troubling for us Plainfielders, they were still not yet big enough for national TV news. I found a New York Times newspaper from that July 1967 weekend. It reported that the Israeli military shot down three Egyptian war planes. The Viet Cong in South Vietnam had attacked the large U.S. air base at Da Nang; 42 of our warplanes had been damaged, and many of our soldiers were left dead and wounded. At the same time, the Newark riot was in full motion and the body count was climbing. There was not a word mentioned about Plainfield. Again, there was no social media as we understand it now. So the question must be asked—how would people from Virginia, Georgia, and Tennessee learn of our problem? I had no doubt: those guys were summoned to Plainfield, and they had a mission, and I feared serious trouble for my city.

The Plainfield Police Department of the 1960s didn't really have to deal with big crime. They issued traffic tickets. They were passively present at football games and high school graduations. They'd stand in the middle of intersections in downtown Plainfield and direct traffic during busy Saturdays. Oh, every once in a while they'd stop a bar fight, or investigate a robbery. The point is, there was no way they were prepared to handle leftover internal problems from the night before *and* all of the outside trouble that paraded in front of my house that Sunday afternoon.

And more trouble was coming.

******

Since there was no school for me during the summer, the daily, casual contact I had with white friends was missing. Once the semester was over in June, I essentially didn't see anyone from school again until September. Since we lived so close to Piscataway, there were a couple of white families along our street. However, there were no young people in any of those homes. That meant I had no direct way of understanding how white people were feeling or reacting to the events in our city. I could guess that they were just as nervous and as upset as my family was.

Later, when I had a chance to speak to white friends, I learned that not only were they as worried as our family, but many of them were also angry. A lot of white folks felt the disorderly young blacks displayed a lack of appreciation for the "privilege" of living in Plainfield. And there were even some white folks who believed the police were not doing enough, so they felt it was up to them to fight back and regain control of "their town." Now, there was no organized anti-black group in Plainfield at that time. However, white folks had their grapevine and rumor mill too. And some people felt it was time to bring in their version of outside agitators.

A motorcycle gang known as the Pagans either were asked or decided on their own to get involved with "the Plainfield problem." The Pagans, who were created in 1959, had been officially listed by the FBI as an "outlaw motorcycle gang." As they grew in members over the years, the Pagans and the Hell's Angels motorcycle gang would clash. In addition, the fun-loving Pagans also got involved in other light-hearted activities like connections with the Mafia and a deep appreciation for the Nazis.

The Nazis!

If you saw a number "5" on a member's denim jacket, that was their homage to Nazi traditions.

Well, a group of those lovely gentlemen came to Plainfield on that Sunday afternoon. Were they summoned? Probably. Again, it's unlikely they heard about the city's troubles through media, especially since they were constantly on the move.

That there was white anxiety, I could understand. I could also understand why longtime white residents of Plainfield did not feel that the Plainfield Police, alone, were adequate to handle a large-scale problem. I'm also sure decent white people would neither want nor ask for the Pagans to be running loose in their city, as I'm sure decent black people did not call or desire angry outside agitators to roam the streets of Plainfield. Nevertheless, both nefarious groups were there. Someone called them in. And before the day was over, they would both add to the trouble in Plainfield.

The potential for a restart of Saturday night's violence was ratcheting up by the hour. But it took an exponential step up when a dangerous theft occurred that day.

I mentioned that Plainfield was surrounded by smaller cities. One of those quiet, smaller cities to the west of Plainfield was Middlesex. With a population of approximately 13,000 and less than four square miles, it was not very large. However, it did have areas of manufacturing. Oddly, for a place so tranquil, I was surprised to learn that a company in Middlesex produced M1 automatic carbine rifles. Ironically, the small factory was called the Plainfield Machine Company. But in truth, it was an arms producer, probably in some way connected to the war in Vietnam. Undoubtedly, someone in Plainfield knew about the place. Because on that Sunday, July 16th, a group from Plainfield broke into that factory and stole 46 of those rifles. It didn't take long to get those lethal weapons the 8.5 miles back to Plainfield and into the hands of reckless people ready to use them. When the Plainfield Police were informed of the theft, they freaked. And they had reason for their angst: within hours of the theft, reports of automatic gunfire within that 14-block hot zone were coming in constantly.

The mayhem had returned.

But it was worse than Friday and Saturday combined. Stores in and outside of that 14-block area were being broken into, looted, and set on fire. Cars were being turned over and lit up. People were being injured in the wild moving melee. Mayor Hetfield, who by now was involved in minute-by-minute decisions, took the advice of the police commanders and ordered the 14-block area to be cordoned off. They would put a total effort into keeping the craziness in that area. However, the mayor and his advisors also made the decision not to go into that area unless absolutely necessary. They felt it was just too dangerous considering the possibility that many lawless individuals were now armed with military weapons and seemingly not hesitant to use them.

The city might have thought they had contained the disorder to that 14-block area, but they hadn't. It had spread to a much wider area of the West End. A clothes cleaner on West Third Street and the popular Mignella's Cleaners on West Fourth Street and Spooner Avenue were broken into and the clothing was stolen. The wonderful grocery Franky's, across the street from the Neighborhood House, was looted and set on fire. Both of those stores were outside of the cordoned-off area. Even the Plainfield Fire Department was under attack. The fortress-like main headquarters located on Central Avenue was relatively safe (although a store right next to it was attacked and looted). However, there were two smaller remote locations strategically placed to better protect the city. The Netherwood branch on the East End had an engine company. That unit was completely out of harm's way. However, the engine company in the West End was located on the corner of West Third Street and Bergen Street—that unit was under siege. Earlier in the evening, those firefighters had tried to put out blazes in their area, but they soon came under rock-and-bottle attack. Eventually, the engine company captain and his five-member crew were essentially chased back to their station, where they barricaded themselves. Soon, gunfire surrounded their remote station deep in the West End. They could neither leave safely nor feel safe inside—they were trapped.

My home was 1.5 miles away from that 14-block hot zone. However, we were less than a half-mile from that fire station.

It had been about six hours since the parade of outside agitators had entered our city. And sure enough, what I had feared had happened—things had exploded in Plainfield. Our normal quiet Sunday evening that would have included watching *The Ed Sullivan Show* and *Bonanza* was interrupted. All eight of us, Mom and Dad and six kids, were in our large living room near the TV when we heard gunshots coming from the general direction of our backyard. Mom and Dad ordered us all to the floor. Dad turned off the TV while Mom turned off the lights. Of all the things that happened during those days of unrest in Plainfield, those moments with my family remain the most personal. For the first time in my life, I heard live gunfire. And for the first time as a family, we were all in danger at the same time.

Now, while on the floor, I tried doing some quick detective work in my head. We lived in a very residential area. There were no commercial stores immediately near our house. So what were the targets of those shots? Were people with guns now shooting at anybody or any car that passed by them? Or were they just randomly firing shots in the air?

We didn't have a basement. There was the ground floor with the living room, kitchen, and a couple of bedrooms and there was an upstairs with two more bedrooms. I'm not sure who gave the order, but it was decided that it was safer upstairs than down. So, we all started crawling toward the steps. We made it past the bathroom and a bedroom. Yes, I was scared, but I was equally amazed to see Mom and Dad on the floor with us. I never saw my parents even sit on the floor, let alone crawl on it. Having them down there with us was as bizarre as if you could imagine Abraham Lincoln and Mother Theresa crawling on a floor; but there they were. Gunshots were still being fired as we started up the steps on our bellies. At the top of the steps on the second floor was a window that faced the backyard. There was no curtail, drapes, or blinds on that small window. So we all knew we had to stay below that window as we reached the second floor. One of my brothers and one of my sisters had made it past that window safely. But as my baby brother, Peter, reached the window, he suddenly stood up, looked out of it, and said, "I don't see anything." Cursing was not common in our house when we were growing up, especially when we were children. However, on that Sunday evening, Peter received a chorus of profanity from my father that included telling him to get his six-year-old butt back on the floor. Eventually, we all made it to the second floor. We stayed there in those two bedrooms until way past midnight as the turmoil continued outside.

What was happening at the same time in other parts of the West End would change the character of Plainfield forever.

9 THE DARK, THE DEVIL, AND DEATH

On April 5th, 1847, Plainfield first took form as a township. One-hundred-twenty years, three months, and eleven days later, that village, now a prosperous city, was experiencing the worst day of its existence.

On Sunday, July 16th, 1967, the northwest sector of the West End was in chaos. Stores were being robbed and looted, missiles were being thrown at moving cars, guns were fired at people and places. There were six firefighters locked in their West End firehouse trying to stay alive. And as bad as all of that was, the 14-block hot zone was now a warzone. It was so dangerous that the police refused to enter it.

A section of the city had been surrendered to

anarchy.

Just about every member of the Plainfield Police Department was on duty. They intended to protect the downtown, white residential areas and keep rioters from entering or leaving the warzone.

When growing up, and still to this day, if I were to see a lone police car with its emergency lights on and a single officer inside or outside of the vehicle intentionally blocking passage to a street, I, along with most Americans, would not challenge that officer. As a matter of fact, we'd automatically stay away. The Plainfield Police Department, stretched to the limits, had created a perimeter around the warzone. That effort took a lot of vehicles and officers; therefore, many of the check points were manned by single officers and their patrol car. Those in charge of trying to manage the situation thought that was adequate.

On that Sunday evening, 39-year-old Officer John V. Gleason was ordered to man the corner of South Second Street and Plainfield Avenue. His job was not to go into the warzone, but rather to keep others from entering it and to alert fellow officers if a large group attempted to spread the violence outward.

As Officer Gleason dutifully and courageously manned his position alone, a group of white young men, possibly mixed with members of the Pagans bike gang, moved toward his checkpoint in an attempt to combat a "mob of Negroes," as they were described. At the same time, a large contingent of black people were also nearby and approaching his checkpoint, but from a different direction. The white group looked like they were trying to get in; the black group appeared to be trying to get out.

Officer Gleason was the only authority, the only hint of law and order, separating the two forces. Soon, the white group spotted the much larger black group. At that point, most of those white folks retreated north back to West Front Street and comparative safety. However, there were one or two stragglers who were spotted by a young black man named Bobby Lee Williams. Mr. Williams caught up to those white guys and attempted to hit them with a hammer.

As to what happened next—I found the following explanation in an official court document:

"The officer [Gleason] sought to arrest one Bobby Lee Williams, who allegedly had attempted to strike some boys with a hammer. As the officer sought to make the arrest, spectators threw sundry missiles at him. In response to some movement by Williams, who still had the hammer, the officer fired his weapon, wounding Williams. Thereupon a mob came at the officer. The officer tried to escape, but after a pursuit involving a considerable distance, he was brought down. Members of the mob inflicted a savage beating which continued until he died."

More details were given by eyewitness Courier News reporter David Hardy:

"When the white youths saw the mob of Negroes, they fled. But it was too late for Gleason. He tried to run, but the Negroes began closing in on him from all directions. He drew his pistol and in panic fired into the group. Young Robby Williams fell to the ground with three bullets in his guts. Screaming epithets, the Negroes swarmed over Gleason, knocking him to the ground. I stood and watched. A Negro woman standing next to me screamed 'Kill that white! Kill him!'"

Another Courier News correspondent, Paul Tharp, also at the scene, reported this:

"I retched when the kid slammed the steel grocery cart into Officer John Gleason's already bloody face… Feet stomped into him, jagged bottles cut him, fists hammered at him, rocks pelted him. Propped up on one elbow, Gleason pleadingly raised his hand. But he found no mercy. A foot kicked him in the back of the head."

Reporter David Hardy continued:

"In the scuffle, someone grabbed Gleason's gun from his hand and shot him as he lay on the ground. Then the rest of the mob began to kick him and beat him with anything they could get their hands on."

There were police officers a few blocks away manning their own checkpoints. Keep in mind everything was crazy that night. So, it took a while for them to notice a disturbance within the disturbance. When officers tried to radio Gleason and received no response, they called for back-up. In a few minutes, a convoy of police cars headed toward where Gleason should have been. As the mass of sirens approached, the deadly mob took off in every direction. When the team of cops arrived at the scene they found, to their horror, the bloody body of a fellow police officer on the pavement. The rescue squad was called for Gleason and Williams. Separate ambulances raced them to the Muhlenberg Hospital. Williams was in critical condition and taken directly to surgery. Officer Gleason was pronounced dead at 8:45 p.m. that Sunday evening.

A nurse on duty at the hospital that night, who later became a friend of mine, was there when Gleason was rolled in. She described the moment to me: "I had never seen anything like that in my life. He was just a pile of mush, every bone in his body was broken. He was unrecognizable."

I'm against capital punishment with the exception of two actions—the murder of a witness to a crime, and the murder of a police officer. When you harm an officer, you are harming the public. If a person would kill a police officer, the person wouldn't hesitate to kill you. If you have a problem with a rogue officer, we have an elaborate legal system that offers many avenues to resolve a complaint.

The mob that attacked Officer Gleason was beyond reasonable, respectable control. They were aflame from the days of agitation leading up to that point. They were livid with any and all white folks. They had been fed hostile encouragement from TV reports of the Newark riot and the deaths of many black people by police gunfire. I am also convinced they were egged on by outside agitators who ratcheted the intensity to a deadly level. It was hot outside, many had been drinking. And in a perverse way, many found it exciting to be out on the streets at night running amok.

So, when that mob ran into the group of bikers and white dudes, any sort of individual thinking, reasoning, or self-control gave way to "groupthink." And when that happens, no one person is in command, no one person takes responsibility, and it takes very little provocation for a leaderless group to act recklessly. Add in situational anger, heavy doses of stupidity, and just a touch of pure evil, and you have a lethal brew. Poor Officer Gleason, a lone sentry and a white face, was surrounded by that sea of toxicity, engulfed, and devoured.

******

Late Sunday night—a police officer had been murdered; many innocent men, women, and even children had been wounded by gunshots. Buildings were on fire, armed rioters were in control of fourteen city blocks, and six firemen were trapped in a fire station in fear of losing their lives. It was a complete and utter nightmare.

Plainfield put out a desperate call for help and the cavalry came.

All the cities surrounding Plainfield sent police officers.

The New Jersey State Police sent detachments of troopers.

And the National Guard was ordered in by the governor.

Now, after midnight, with a force of more than 200 police officers and 100 soldiers, plans were made to take back the streets. The first thing Mayor Hetfield and his command team felt they had to do was to rescue the trapped firefighters. A heavily-armed contingent aided by an armored military vehicle set out for the firehouse. That task force had to dodge sniper bullets, Molotov cocktails, bricks, and rocks on the way there, but they made it and got the captain and his five firefighters out safely.

© 2017 Google Inc, used with permission.

As for the 14-block warzone, the authorities decided not to attempt to enter that nest of chaos at night. Rather, they would reinforce their encirclement of the area to keep the trouble contained until morning. Anarchy was allowed to reign within the zone. Residents trapped in the cordoned-off area described Sunday night and early Monday morning as living in hell. They couldn't sleep because of the constant shooting and fear of fire. They watched as prowling gangs of black youths shot out streetlights, broke into stores, and damaged cars, confident that the police would not respond. The only thing those innocent victims could do was to barricade themselves in their homes, and then hope and pray for the best.

10 "INSURRECTION"

"Insurrection"—that was how Mayor Hetfield described the situation in Plainfield on Monday, July 17th, 1967.

For the West End of Plainfield, that was pretty much the truth. A resentment against police and civil authority that had been kindling for quite a while was now in full motion. Nonetheless, the Mayor and his advisors now felt it was time to start the process of taking back the West End and, in particular, the warzone. First, the New Jersey National Guard was to take over for the Plainfield Police and surround the cordoned off-area. Their orders—no one leaves, and no one goes in. From Front Street to Seventh, from Madison Avenue to Plainfield Avenue, the entire place was considered a crime scene. However, the actual patrol area for the troops was extended almost a mile west to Clinton Avenue. Those soldiers, who patrolled in jeeps and armored personnel carriers, were well-armed and serious about their assignment.

The mayor then initiated a list of actions to help bring calm back to the area. There was a curfew immediately put into effect. No one was allowed on the streets from 10 p.m. to 6 a.m. All liquor stores and bars were to be closed until further notice. The mayor also recommended cities near the Plainfield border to close their liquor stores. Plainfield's summer schools and playgrounds were closed. Bus routes were detoured around the cordoned-off area and mail deliveries were suspended in the West End. In addition, any calls to the fire department for help would not be answered until the police could confirm that there was indeed a fire. More than eighteen calls to the fire department were left unanswered under those conditions.

Downtown Plainfield was practically shut down. Although officially just outside the "warzone," it was still too close to the trouble for most storeowners and shoppers. What should have been a busy and profitable Monday was reduced to locked doors and no customers. Even the most stable and secure institutions like the Plainfield Trust State National Bank (now PNC Bank) closed all six branches in Plainfield.

The next step would be the hardest—to actually enter that 14-block warzone and put an end to the rebellion. However, with all of those stolen weapons allegedly distributed to people in the zone, along with hundreds of reports of gunfire, the police would have to move in slowly and cautiously. Around 10 a.m. on Monday morning, a heavily armed force of local and state police supported by the military entered the area. Initial radio reports from that task force to police headquarters indicated that gunshots could still be heard. Although the streets were basically empty, groups of black teenagers could still be seen roaming around. The police force found entire areas littered with trash, almost every store either completely looted or burned out, and many overturned and burned-out cars.

Nevertheless, the task force pushed on. By the afternoon, the police probes had looked into all sectors of the 14-block warzone. Soon thereafter, squadrons of police and military units patrolled the area constantly.

When my supervisor at the playground called and told me that all the playgrounds in the city were closed, I wondered what had happened on Sunday that would cause such an unprecedented action. When our Monday Courier Newspaper arrived, I got my answers:

"*'Insurrection' Rakes City*"

and

"Mob Stomps Wounded Policeman to Death"

I lost my breath as I read those headlines; it was almost surreal learning what had taken place in Plainfield overnight. After reading everything that had happened, I decided I wanted to see first-hand what was going on.

I grabbed my little brother Peter and we started walking east to his school, Clinton Elementary; it would take only five minutes to get there. Now, as we approached the school, I didn't know exactly what I was looking for. Perhaps we might see what had been hit from all the gunfire last night. Maybe we would see the results of all the burning and looting. As we approached the corner of Clinton Avenue and West Fourth Street, we found a military jeep and four solders. All of them were helmeted, in their green combat uniforms, and with rifles with bayonets on them. I had seen soldiers on television and movies plenty of times. I had seen them in dress uniforms in Plainfield's annual Fourth of July parade, but I had never seen real soldiers in combat uniforms upfront and personal. Before long, two of those solders moved toward us. One of them lowered his weapon in our direction. For the first and only time in my life, a person was about to aim a gun at me. But before that happened, the other soldiers yelled, "Turn around, go back home! Go home, now!"

Now, I'm as peaceful and as respectful of the law as anyone could be. I'm the furthest thing from a troublemaker. But I have to admit, I didn't like soldiers telling me to go home, it just seemed wrong. Nevertheless, Peter and I turned around and returned home. If nothing else, we had a juicy story to tell the rest of the family.

My subtle resentment of what the soldiers shouted to my brother and me was nothing compared to the open hostility between the residents of that 14-block warzone and the heavy police presence. Phone calls from friends living in the warzone revealed that tensions in the cordoned-off area remained extremely high. As the sun started setting on that Monday, shots rang out from various spots of the warzone and all over the West End. Now, I'm sure my mother's friends and many other older people felt comfortable with the police and military attempting to restore order. However, the young folks were still in charge, and they didn't like the idea of all those cops in their hood.

The frontline police reported that enmity to their superiors.

The mayor, the chief of police, the state police commander, and the military commander all felt they still had a dangerous environment to contend with. Whatever tactical scenario they dreamt up to make things better was confronted by the reality of all of those stolen weapons presumably in the hands of the rioters.

So, they came up with a very controversial plan—to search all the houses in the cordoned-off zone for the stolen weapons. On paper, it might have sounded like a good idea: remove the guns and the sniping, gunfire, and extreme danger should stop. But having predominantly white cops go into a hostile area searching for guns was going to cause trouble. Also, there was a legal problem with the idea. Normally, you need a search warrant to enter a person's home to look for items. But in order to get that warrant, you have to demonstrate "probable cause." That would require detective work, and that would take time. Hetfield and his team didn't feel they had the luxury of time; they wanted those guns off the streets immediately.

So Mayor Hetfield, who was in constant contact with Governor Hughes, requested the assistance of New Jersey Attorney General Arthur J. Sills and Paul N. Ylvisaker of the New Jersey Department of Community Affairs to determine what steps could be legally taken. They drove to Plainfield late Monday to meet with the mayor and his advisors.

In the meantime, there were many pastors, church members, and other community leaders like the Lattimore brothers and Mr. Judkins at work behind the scenes trying to calm things down. In addition to those gentlemen, there were two other black leaders who made headlines during the riot. One was Charles Miller, the vice chairman of the Plainfield Human Relations Commission. He was doing his best to handle things. Another equally potent black leader during those days of turmoil who, more or less, appointed himself to speak for the rioters was young Linward Cathcart.

While Everett Lattimore, Mr. Judkins, and Mr. Miller were more like Martin Luther King in their approach to civil rights issues, Linward Cathcart, in my opinion, was more like Malcolm X. When the mayor and all his lieutenants were threatening to use force as a remedy to the rioters, Mr. Cathcart didn't mind threatening back. I've observed something interesting during my lifetime about black leaders in America and how white folks react to them. White people are more inclined to deal with a Martin Luther King type of leader than with a Malcolm X. MLK was a highly-intelligent saint with a godly vision and mission of good for all. It was certainly easier to come to the table and make a deal with him. Dr. King was a threat to the "status quo" but not a violent one. On the other hand, white folks in power do not like the Malcolm Xs, the Al Sharptons, and the Louis Farrakhans. I've sat with too many white friends who did not hesitate to express their honest disdain for these men. White folks have found it hard to understand how those men, and other angry black leaders, have become heroic symbols in the black community.

Well, here's a clue.

For many years, black people had to read in newspapers and see on television the gross injustice put upon them by the racist, suppressive systems in the Southern parts of the United States. Yes, there was a gathering of excellent black leaders who fought peacefully against such oppression. People like the great intellectual W.E.B. Du Bois became so infuriated with the American capitalist system (which he insisted was the cause of racism in our country), and after witnessing lynchings and all sorts of atrocities against blacks, that he joined the communist party. He didn't like the violence and evils of communism, but he did like the philosophical idea of fair and equal opportunity for ALL, which was the original core of the communist socialist system.

But Du Bois, Booker T. Washington, and other early leaders were determined to be peaceful in their approach to change. However, now in the late 1960s, there were a growing number of those who felt it was time to fight back one way or another. If you couldn't take up a gun, at least get in the face of the oppressive authority and give them as many heated words as they poured on the black community.

Twenty-nine-year-old Linward Cathcart got in the face of what he saw as an oppressive authority. He was the Al Sharpton of Plainfield during the riots. He bravely went to the heart of the warzone and spoke to everyone who had something to say. He made the Neighborhood House on West Fourth Street his headquarters. He spoke on behalf of the rioters, the victims of the riot, and the long-term racial problems of Plainfield.

My brother Peter knew Mr. Cathcart's son, who was also named Linward. I actually met both father and son when I volunteered at a youth center in Plainfield. As I recall, neither son nor father were physically big guys, but both carried themselves with distinction. The son was polite and followed instructions better than the average kid. The father shook hands and thanked folks for any courtesy extended to his family. Personally, I am not one to advocate violence to solve a problem, and I'm sure Mr. Cathcart wasn't for violence either. But I have to admit, at times, I admired and appreciated the tough voice who would stand up for the people. From overhearing my mother's phone calls, I knew she and many others had the highest regard for Mr. Cathcart. So with that endorsement, he was OK for me.

Mr. Cathcart, somehow, learned of the meeting with the mayor and the state representatives at City Hall. He went there and insisted on being part of the meeting, and he was granted access. Mr. Cathcart, Mayor Hetfield, Plainfield Police chief Donald Payne, the state attorney general, and a team of assistants were determined to work all night to reach a workable agreement that would hopefully stop further violence.

That was the ray of hope that closed a difficult Monday night in Plainfield.

11 "THE TRUCE"

By early Tuesday morning, July 18th, the team that had worked overnight to reach a peace had found one. It was simply called "the truce."

This was the core of it:

1. About 160 people had been arrested so far. Mr. Cathcart requested that twelve of those arrested, with relatively small, non-violent charges against them, be released immediately as a positive sign.

2. The heavy police and military presence would be removed from the 14-block warzone.

3. Since so many stores had been destroyed and the area cordoned off, there was a shortage of food in the West End. Mr.

Cathcart wanted food delivered to the area immediately.

4. There would be an investigation into the grievances of the rioters. Those grievances were very similar to problems experienced in riots across the country—police brutality, better living conditions, and better opportunities.

5. In exchange for the above, Mr. Cathcart would get the rioters to return the 46 automatic weapons stolen from the Plainfield Machine Company building in Middlesex.

Those were the basics of the truce, but it was not universally accepted. Most of the members of the Plainfield Police Department hated it. They described the truce as a "sell out." They saw the agreement as trading prisoners for guns, and they found that unpalatable. I could understand the police position; they had a dead comrade, and they wanted some sort of immediate justice for him. But cooler heads prevailed—Cathcart and the other community leaders were given time to find and return the weapons.

So, the truce went into effect.

Police and National Guard units were cautiously pulled out of the warzone. Twelve prisoners were selected and put in police cars to be returned from Elizabeth, New Jersey. The Plainfield jail was relatively small and certainly not equipped to handle all the arrests made during the riot. So most of the prisoners had been taken to the large Union County Jail in Elizabeth.

As the authorities did their part, Cathcart and other community leaders branched out into the community and started their search for the guns. However, even as the truce started, there were still reports of gunfire in the warzone. Nevertheless, responsible black leaders continued their attempts to find those weapons. One of those leaders was a former Plainfield High School sports star and Olympic champion, Milt Campbell. He flew in from California once he heard of the trouble his hometown was having. He was allowed to go right into the heart of the warzone. He talked with many individuals, some who were guilty of crimes and many who were innocent. Campbell did not try to distinguish between them; he just listened and tried tirelessly to bring peace to the area. At the end of the day, his observations were that most black folks in the warzone wanted peace and normalcy. He also firmly felt that outside agitators were the key figures behind all the trouble. He also believed that trying to recapture those 46 stolen automatic weapons was a lost cause. After listening to many, he felt the agitators had taken most of the guns with them when they left the city.

Nevertheless, the search for the weapons

continued all day Tuesday. In addition, the police and military searched every car entering or leaving the troubled West End. My father, when he returned from his job in Cranford on that Tuesday evening, told us that he was stopped and told to get out of the car while he and his car were searched by the military and police. He said he had to go through that procedure four times as he drove through Plainfield that morning and returned in the evening.

12 "UNPRECEDENTED"

Wednesday, July 19th, 1967.

The truce had been in place for twenty-four hours. Violence had been greatly reduced; however, it had not totally stopped. The twelve prisoners, who were part of the truce deal, had been delivered and released. Cathcart and other community leaders had searched for the weapons. But none were found.

I had been essentially locked in my home for three days. The playground was still closed, so there was no work. A good portion of the West End of Plainfield was still surrounded by National Guard troops. So, everyone in my home was limited to where they could go. Even with all the restrictions and police patrols, occasional gunshots could be heard in the distance, so there were still problems.

My mother was getting horror stories from her friends living in the warzone. Mrs. Blair and Mrs. Brunner reported that some teenager, running from the cops, had tried to break into their home late last night. The person couldn't get through the thick side door and eventually left. Those sisters and their neighbors were tired of living in fear.

Mayor Hetfield and his command team had waited a full day without one weapon turned in. They decided it was time to show that they meant business. In order to do a search for weapons in the warzone, they were going to need more police and soldiers. On that Wednesday morning, more state police and another contingent of military units poured into Plainfield. Hundreds of soldiers were now stationed in the city and ready to move into the warzone and do something never done before during any riot in America so far. They were going to do a door-to-door search for and seizure of weapons—*without warrants*.

The right of the people to be secure in their persons, houses, papers, and effects, against unreasonable searches and seizures, shall not be violated, and no Warrants shall issue, but upon probable cause, supported by Oath or affirmation, and particularly describing the place to be searched, and the persons or things to be seized.

That passage of text is directly from the Fourth Amendment of the Constitution of the United States. The mayor and his advisors were intent on ignoring it if Cathcart and other leaders could not produce the weapons by noon on Wednesday. That plan, which on the surface seemed to ignore the Constitution, was OK'd by Arthur Sills, the state attorney general, who was still in Plainfield. The plan was even reviewed by Governor Hughes, and he OK'd it after he declared a state of emergency in Plainfield. That declaration was probably the legal loophole they were going to use to try to make such a technically illegal mass search legitimate.

Mr. Cathcart and the other community leaders certainly tried their best to follow up on their part of the deal. But after a while, Cathcart reported to Mr. Sills that it would probably take a lot longer to find the weapons. The noon deadline passed with no delivery of the 46 stolen rifles. Curiously, no action was taken by the city at that hour. However, the massive search team was gearing up to go in. Charles Miller, Plainfield's Human Relations Commission vice chairman, was alarmed by a frenzied, gung-ho attitude among some members of the military and law enforcement. The Courier News reported this comment from Mr. Miller: "If any National Guardsman or police officer shoots, without provocation, I'll work against you, not with you." Mr. Miller directed that statement to an officer of the National Guard. Other community leaders from the warzone promised "massive retaliation" should the police and military start indiscriminately shooting people (again, keep in mind the Newark riot was still fresh in people's minds. There had been many TV interviews of black people in Newark who claimed that at the height of the riot, the police and military were just shooting people at random).

******

It was past 2 p.m. and still no delivery of the stolen guns.

Mayor Hetfield honestly or naively felt that the weapons were still in the cordoned-off area, so he felt he had to act. So, he gave the word to go. Under the command of State Police Colonel David B. Kelly, a heavily armed force of 400 military, state police, and local police officers moved into the 14-block warzone and started a house-to-house search for the missing weapons.

Unfortunately, by 1967, the big city riots, weekly reports of body counts from the Vietnam War, and tragedies from around the world were becoming the norm for the media. For TV network news divisions to send a news team to an incident, something had to be unique about the event. Well, in Newark, the story was about the high death count and the closeness to New York City.

The Plainfield riot, although a disaster for Plainfielders, was not big news nationally until two things happened: first, the brutal murder of Officer Gleason; and then, the house-by-house search. Regrettably, police officers had been killed in other riots. An officer was killed in the Newark riot along with a firefighter. However, it was the vicious nature of Officer Gleason's murder that caught the news networks' attention. But oddly, even more than that, it was the unprecedented search that also piqued their interest.

I was an avid TV newsaholic, even as a child. My favorite source was TV news legend Walter Cronkite; I watched him constantly, Monday through Friday, for years. I was very familiar with the style and format in which he presented his 30-minute program. On that Wednesday evening, I was parked in front of the TV set when the *CBS Evening News with Walter Cronkite* came on. He always started the program by telling his viewers where he had sent his best correspondents. Sending just one of his celebrated reporters to a location gave the story importance. To my surprise, Mr. Cronkite announced that not one but two correspondents would be reporting from Plainfield, New Jersey. It was the strangest feeling to be impressed and depressed at the same time. I watched as Walter Cronkite started his nationally-watched program with video footage of columns of military vehicles rolling through the streets of Plainfield as combat helicopters flew overhead.

Lead by Col. Kelly, who had been given total authority of the search by the governor, the hunt started at the West End Gardens apartment complex. The CBS News cameras (along with the other TV networks and other media) caught the images of soldiers with bayonetted rifles and police with machine guns and shotguns, side by side. Some of them were even wearing gas masks. Teams of them were seen going in and out of apartments as the black residents were ordered out of their homes. Although there were leaders of the black community scattered among those armed units as observers, the search was not welcomed by the residents of the West End Gardens, and it made many of them furious.

For a search of that entire warzone to be completely legal, a warrant would have to be sought, approved, and issued for each of the 128 apartments and hundreds of homes in that 14-block zone. Mayor Hetfield, Governor Hughes, and State Attorney General Sills thought they could bypass that constitutional procedure—and they were doing it with the nation watching.

Of course, nowadays, all the actions of the soldiers and police would have been recorded by folks with their cell phone cameras and put on social media almost instantly. But that ability was 40 years in the future. So even with a lot of media on site, the reports coming out of the area were conflicting. Some apartment residents complained that their doors were broken open for no reason and their possessions were damaged and thrown about. Milt Campbell, an official observer, said that he personally saw doors broken and a considerable amount of damage inside some apartments. Linward Cathcart, another on-site witness, reported multiple apartments "torn up" and many people upset. Councilman Everett Lattimore said that the manner in which National Guard troops conducted themselves did not help the overall conditions at the West End Gardens.

Curiously, after about an hour into what was going to be an all-day operation, the search was stopped. During that time, only three of the stolen weapons were recovered. Strangely, no one seemed to know at the time who exactly called off the search. When asked by a group of reporters about the sudden end to the search, a seemingly annoyed Col. Kelly replied that the plan was to only search the West End Gardens apartments and a few other places designated by the Plainfield Police Department.

Many did not believe him.

When Governor Hughes was questioned about the abbreviated pursuit of the weapons, he replied, "The search—that was a duty and necessity—was concluded because it was completed." When asked by reporters if the people who had possession of the stolen weapons would be arrested, the governor's responded, "We are primarily interested in the guns and not in arrests." He went on to say that the policy of no arrest did not include the investigation of the murder of Officer

Gleason.

Whatever the reasons, the unprecedented search that was called "logical" by some and a gross violation of constitutional liberties by others was halted for the moment. The armed forces were pulled out of the warzone. But they still cordoned off the area and continued searching every car going in and out of the 14-blocks and the extended zone.

I had three opinions then and now about that search.

First, it never would have happened in an area that was predominantly white. It just wouldn't; I don't think I have to go into the obvious reasons. Second, the local cops wanted to avenge Officer Gleason. I don't think police officers should have had that mentality, but to be fair, I can understand the position. Third, I think a lot of those soldiers and cops expected and wanted a massive shootout. They thought some hardcore group of individuals was holed up somewhere in the West End Gardens with all of the weapons; when those individuals saw that they were surrounded, they would barricade themselves in a couple of apartments and have a shootout.

As crazy as that might seem, future tragedies in Waco, Texas; Ruby Ridge, Idaho; and Philadelphia, with the MOVE confrontations and shootouts (where cops fired thousands of bullets and used a bomb against black suspects), verify that when the authorities arrive, as they did at the West End Gardens, heavily armed in massive numbers, with armored personnel carriers, gas masks, and helicopters, they expect and are prepared for a lot of gunplay.

Yes, there was a lot of resentment, but no violence. OK, what to do next? The mayor, the governor, and the military and police forces, along with legal teams, had to figure that out and quickly. The majority of the rifles were still missing. Would the search continue?

13 "TRANSITION"

Thursday, July 20th, 1967. That day in Plainfield started very similarly to the day before. There was still a large police and military presence in the West End. The odious possibility of more house-to-house searches still hung in the air. Curfews were still in effect; many places and businesses remained closed. The warzone was still cordoned off, cars were still being searched going in and out of that zone, and hostilities from each side remained high.

Nevertheless, there were a couple of things different about that Thursday.

First, a lot of people who had been arrested over the last four days were now facing judges. Some individuals charged with minor offenses that would have been hard to prove were let go. Those accused of carrying weapons, resisting arrest, or possessing stolen property were given bail and court dates. Most of these legal proceedings took place in Elizabeth with Union County Judge John L. Ard, who was acting on behalf of the Plainfield judges. The Plainfield court system could not handle the more than 100 arrests. So many of the prisoners had been shipped to the County Jail in Elizabeth. According to Everett Lattimore, some of those Union County Jail guards had been verbally and physically abusive to the Plainfield prisoners. In a statement to the Courier News, Mr. Lattimore said, "I have received complaints from prisoners that they were abused at the Union County Jail. They were call 'niggers' and were jabbed with guns by the guards." At the same time, Mr. Lattimore said that some of the prisoners gave the guards a hard time. They verbally abused the police, and one prisoner spit in the face of a cop. Those incidents were symbolic of the total lack of respect of many young folks towards the police, and the lack of respect of the police towards those young black people.

The other important event, a more sorrowful and solemn event on that Thursday, was the funeral of Officer John Gleason. Police from all over, including state police and Newark police, dignitaries, family, and friends were all part of an almost 100-car cortege that started at Plainfield High School, traveled to Higgins Funeral Home on West 8th Street to pick up the body, and then proceeded to St. Mary's Church on West 6th Street near Liberty Street for the service. Ironically, St. Mary's Church was inside the 14-block warzone. But the security for the funeral was extensive, and there were no incidents. Once the funeral was over, the long motorcade passed by Plainfield Police Headquarters and then to a cemetery in Woodbridge, New Jersey.

******

Meanwhile, black folks in the cordoned-off area were getting restless. But not in a violent way. Those who had nothing to do with the troubles were tired of their streets and homes looking like a hurricane went through them. So, many started cleaning their lawns and streets on their own. Because of the damage to all the local food stores, folks without cars, and no bus service, there were many families running low on food and with no way to get more. As negotiated by Linward Cathcart and others, a federal agency used the Neighborhood House on West Fourth Street as a distribution point for free food. Cheese, dried milk, and canned meat were given to adults in the cordoned-off areas. Now, with people being fed, streets getting cleaned, and "peace patrols" on duty (volunteer black citizens wearing white armbands patrolling their own area and helping to keep things quiet), Plainfield experienced its first quiet afternoon and evening in a week. The area was so quiet during that evening that it was described by members of the media as resembling a ghost town. The Plainfield Police, the National Guard, and the State Police were still patrolling the West End. Nevertheless, they reported very few, if any, people out. The ones they did see basically ignored them and went about their business.

14 "RETURN TO NORMALCY"

On Friday, July 21ˢᵗ, 1967, at 8.am., Mayor Hetfield declared the hostilities over.

The military was ordered out of the city. The cordoned area was opened, and police patrols restarted in the troubled area. The State Police stayed in the city, but all the other neighboring police forces were thanked and released. All businesses were opened, including liquor stores, and the curfews were lifted.

As much as it could, Plainfield went back to normal.

I got an early phone call from my supervisor at the playground—since our area (so close to Piscataway) had not been touched by the riots, we would be back to work that Friday. That was great news, as I was really tired of staying at home. I didn't wait for Mr. Crowley's ride; I decided to take my bike to work. While passing through the neighborhoods to Rushmore playground, it occurred to me that if I had not known there had been a riot in the city, it wouldn't have been evident. The only indicator that something was not quite right was a Plainfield Police car that drove by slowly followed by a State Police cruiser. There were two officers in the Plainfield car and four state troopers in their car, and they had their shotguns visibly poking out of their windows.

The day at the playground was part work, but mostly sitting around and talking about the last week of events.

Listening to my coworkers, then later to my friends, family, and my mother's friends—there was a clear theme to their thoughts about the riots. First, almost all thought it was a disgrace. My father was a man of a few words, but when issued, they were usually intense and to the point. "What was the point! Those damned niggers tore up their own damned neighborhoods." That was a direct quote from dear old Dad. He continued: "Why tear up our side of town? If they wanted to do something, let them go and tear up the white people's side of town." Even my God-fearing, church-going mother described the rioters as "those damned fool niggers." I believe her reaction came from listening to dozens of her church friends living in fear during the riot. All of my sources felt that Plainfield could have done a lot to prevent the riots; although Plainfield's historical racial problems were nothing like the folly of Southern states, there were things that needed to be fixed.

Everyone felt that the killing of Officer Gleason was awful, unwarranted, and not part of any civil rights movement, especially my dad. My father had seen lynchings down South as a teenager. He knew how appalling situations could get. My father spoke very little about political or social things. When President Kennedy, Malcolm X, and even Martin Luther King were assassinated, I never heard a word or thought out of him. However, when he went out of his way to describe Gleason's death as "uncalled for," it said a lot to me as to how wrong it was.

My sources also praised and admired Everett Lattimore and Linward Cathcart. They thought the duo represented black people passionately and intelligently and sought the best solutions possible. Mr. Lattimore's ardent pleas for all Plainfielders to mourn the loss of Officer Gleason and to work toward a peaceful recovery were praised by all sides.

There was one unfortunate thing about my sources that summer—none of them were white. I had many white friends, but I had no contact with them during the summer. There were no white kids at the playground and no white folks at my church.

And we, as a family, never went to the Jersey shore. The thought of it was a joke to us. So, I had no white input on those major events. But I could certainly sense that they too had concerns for Plainfield's future. It was going to take a lot of money to restore the West End. Where was that capital going to come from? What bank or financial institution would feel safe putting money into a community that would destroy itself?

One of the complaints by rioters was that there weren't enough opportunities for black folks before the riot. Well, what about all the opportunities lost with the destruction of all the black businesses that did exist in the West End before the riot? Later that Friday, after work, I rode my bike through the troubled areas of the West End. I was shocked. Dozens and dozens of stores and places that had been part of my childhood tapestry were smashed, looted, or burned out. An overwhelming dread besieged me as I continued my survey. But I almost lost it when I saw Franky's grocery store. Burning that good man's place of business was perhaps the most unfair thing I had ever witnessed. I went home after seeing that; I couldn't take any more.

On that Friday, Governor Hughes came out and blamed the riots in Plainfield and Newark on "criminals who hate America and who hate God." Personally, I thought that was one of the stupidest and most naïve statements ever made by a

politician. I was not alone in criticizing the governor
and Mayor Hetfield in their performances. Black
folks felt the mayor was completely out of touch
and out of sync with the black community. Many
thought the governor was also out of touch.
However, a few gave Hughes some credit for his
follow-up remarks. On that first day of peace in
Plainfield, the governor was in Miami Beach,
Florida speaking to a union group. According to the
Associated Press, New Jersey's governor went on
to say, "The criminal participants who ambushed
firemen doing their duty putting out fires, the
killers of children, the mass looters, amounted to
less than one percent of the whole Negro
population of Newark. And in the same way, the
white people who did their best to make the
situation worse—the haters, the advocates of
slaughtering innocent Negroes, were also like that
[Negro] one percent."

That Friday remained quiet in Plainfield.
However, the following Saturday had a few
highlights. Two more of the stolen guns were found
in the former warzone at a small and very old
place—Evergreen Cemetery on Plainfield Avenue.
The Plainfield Police were still looking for those
missing rifles, but in a more passive way. They
looked through the old cemetery and just
happened to find those weapons there near a
tombstone. To their credit, the Plainfield Police and
detectives on the scene collected their evidence
and then moved on. There was no rush back to

combat status—no helmets, gas masks, and shotguns. No, the Plainfield Police wanted only three things for the moment: peace in the city, more of the stolen weapons, and most importantly, the killers of Officer Gleason. They were determined to engage all three objectives.

However, none of the remaining stolen carbine rifles were ever recovered.

Just a block away from the cemetery at the West End Gardens, there were plenty of activities—not police work, but legal work. Convinced that the search of those apartments was constitutionally illegal, teams of lawyers from the local NAACP, the American Civil Liberties Union, and the national NAACP Legal Defense Fund came to the West End Gardens to take statements from everyone whose home was searched. In addition, the legal team was going to seek a court injunction to stop any further searches. It wasn't long before the ACLU of New Jersey filed a million-dollar lawsuit against Governor Hughes on behalf of 66 families living at the West End Gardens. Hughes tried to justify his position by stating the situation was under a state of emergency. Eventually, the case was settled out of court for $40,000. Each of the individual plaintiffs received part of the $40K. The largest amount went to a mother who was in her apartment nursing her baby when the soldiers and troopers smashed the door in and removed her from her home.

There was another organization that expressed anxiety over the riots and their aftermath. It was the Plainfield Area Chamber of Commerce. They were worried that the riot would hurt the social and economic future of Plainfield.

They had no idea how right they were going to be.

******

So that's how the Plainfield riots started and essentially ended, at least as far as I was concerned. Eventually, quite a few people were arrested for the murder of Officer Gleason. And the city did try to repair the social and physical damage of the riots.

I'll attempt to sum all of that up in the final chapter of this book.

But now, on to the racial conflict that tore apart the Plainfield school system.

15 THE PLAINFIELD HIGH SCHOOL RIOT

"HOW IT STARTED"

When I look back to a time of serious changes in our country and my life, without a doubt, it was the 1960s.

Yes, yes, computers, cell phones, drones, huge TVs, and a host of other things have impacted the 21st century. But they don't compare to when America engaged a young new president, the space program, The Beatles, women's liberation, the Vietnam conflict, and the civil rights movement toward racial equality. Trust me, it was a special time.

Of those events, the racial problem hit home the hardest.

However, I was not aware of that problem as a child going to school in Plainfield. To me, my hometown was a terrifically placid place to live. And I was not really aware of race at all. That is, until one day in 1963 when I was twelve. I was walking along the hallways of Maxson Junior High School headed toward my science class taught by a Miss Sliker. While on the way there, I found myself behind three girls who were having a rather loud conversation. They were talking about the racial make-up of their friends. They said things like, "Sheila, who's white, didn't like Ronald, who's black. But her best friend, Ellen, who's white, said she should go out with Jesse, who's black." They kept on naming people and describing their color. Believe it or not, it wasn't until that moment that I stopped and thought about the racial status of my friends. Before that day, Kirby was Kirby, Allen was Allen, Peggy was Peggy, Mildred was Mildred. But then I realized that Kirby was white, Allen was black, Peggy and Mildred were white. That silly, random conversation caused me to do a complete inventory of my friends. I suddenly realized that I was surrounded by white kids and that I had classes that didn't have any other black, Hispanic, or Asian kids in them. And it wasn't until high school that I actually met a Hispanic or Asian kid. Those races were few and far between in Plainfield at the time.

So, I grew up in a town that was predominantly white. But it was also peaceful and friendly, at least to me. At the time, I couldn't recall any overtly racial act aimed at me or anyone I knew. Although I was suddenly made aware of color, it wasn't a problem or any sort of factor in my young life.

Then the riots came to Plainfield.

Transformations came to my peaceful world and many of them were not good.

By the time I was a senior at Plainfield High School, the riots were two years behind us. But emotional wounds of those dark days were far from healed. During those two years, Dr. Martin Luther King had been murdered. That started another round of major city riots across the country. Vietnam was still a bloody mess, and a new president, Richard Nixon, was promising "law and order" and displayed no interest in civil rights.

Yes, the world I lived in had been altered. Nevertheless, my day-to-day life was alright. Being more nerdy than anything else, I was enjoying watching *Lost in Space* on TV, reading *Catcher in the Rye*, and working part-time on the weekends. I was OK.

I was in what many experts considered one of the best high schools in the state. Plainfield High School would be hard, but I had learned from John F. Kennedy that hard is good. So I walked the corridors of Plainfield pleased that I was there. I had solid friends at PHS, many of whom had been with me since elementary school. While there, I think I did something that I'm pretty sure most people didn't do: I viewed my school life and my fellow students through the eyes of a documentary filmmaker. I didn't use a real camera, my mind was my recorder. Every day as I entered PHS, it was like I heard "Camera... Action;" my virtual camera started rolling. To me, every student, teacher, janitor, and staff member was a star of my ongoing movie. I recorded every face; piece of clothing; type of hats, book bags, dresses, shoes—everything. I noticed how the most handsome guys got the prettiest girls. I noted that some of my friends were funny, some were serious. Some of the girls wore really nice clothes, some of the boys wore the same thing all the time. One member of my class carried a big boom box radio everywhere he went. He was "Radio Raheem" twenty years before filmmaker Spike Lee created the character for his movie *Do The Right Thing*. One of my friends was just as ugly as ugly could get, but he was probably the smartest kid in the school. The hallways were alive with every type of kid, all well-meaning and harmless to each other. Scrawny childhood friends who had played war games with me in the park now had muscles and mustaches and played football, wrestled, and swam for the Plainfield Cardinals. The girls—well, the little girls of my early years—had developed in eye-catching ways too.

To me, high school was a vigorous, colorful show. In many ways, it reminded me of my favorite TV program, *Star Trek*. In that world, races of all types got along well together as they pursued a gallant objective. I saw the same racial harmony in the high school with my cerebral camera. And our goals of college and careers seemed gallant enough.

However, I now must admit that my comprehension of good old Plainfield High School was incomplete, because I was recording only what I saw.

I had no idea there were outside influences creating tension within the school. Much like that long train of cars that rolled into Plainfield two years ago, filled with hateful people, or the arrival of the Pagans on that fateful Sunday, there were outside forces trying to sway the hearts and minds of my fellow students. I just didn't notice it. My immediate group of racially-mixed friends gave no indication that there were any problems. But, admittedly, we were all nerdy and focused on intellectual pursuits. Although I was visually captivated by the 1,666 students in the school, I didn't have a pulse on their overall disposition.

Well, if I had the ability to scan and analyze the internal condition of the large student body, my sensors would have reported that the body was developing a fever. Back in July 1967 after the riots, many of the participants of that disaster talked to Everett Lattimore and other adult black leaders and shouted off a list of complaints again the city. Many of those grievances had been brewing for years. Well, I wasn't aware of a similar list of complaints that some black students had against the status quo of the high school. And those grievances had been simmering for a long time.

******

Plainfield High School had a "track system" back then. I'm sure it was officially explained as a systemic way of placing students in classes that would serve their best interests. It did sound good on paper, but in reality, most of the white kids ended up in classes that were college prep, while most of the black kids were directed to classes designed for service careers.

At first I didn't notice this. But in time, it was clear that the best teachers and the most advanced classes were populated mostly by white students. It was also clear that the simpler classes that included wood shop, metal shop, home economics (essentially cooking classes), and auto shop were loaded with black students. If you could have viewed the long corridors of the school or visited the library or cafeteria like I did with my virtual camera, you saw a nice racial balance. However, if you were able to peer into math and science classes at any given time, you would see the racial polarization.

Black students of the early 1960s, who were complacent or unaware of racial strife in America, had by 1969 been fed a massive amount of awareness. Many had also been given potent lessons by tough young black national leaders like H. Rapp Brown, who said, "If America don't come around, we're gonna burn it down;" and fiery Eldridge Cleaver, who said, "You are either part of the solution or part of the problem," and "Too much agreement kills a chat;" and Huey Newton, who said, "The revolution has always been in the hands of the young. The young always inherit the revolution," and "I do not expect the white media to create positive black male images."

Many black teenagers were changing their hairstyles and clothing to reflect a revolution in attitude. TV shows that I grew up with like *The Donna Reed Show*, *Leave it to Beaver*, *Father Knows Best*, and hundreds like them, with their all-white casts depicting a sterile all-white society, were no longer welcomed but resented. All of that new perception of culture and attitude had infected many of the students of Plainfield High School.

My daily recording did note more afros on black students, more African styles worn by the girls, but I just thought it was an interesting sign of our modern times, nothing more.

Another factor that should be considered—the residual effects of the Plainfield riot. Many of the black students at PHS grew up in the psychologically- and physically-traumatized West End. They remembered the armies of police and soldiers, the illegal searches, the blockades of their streets, and being without food and light for days.

The riot also affected many white students too. They were keenly aware that a white policeman was murdered by out-of-control blacks, that their beloved hometown with its tradition values had been altered by the riot, and that its future was threatened by a host of changes. And many white students (and their families) did not welcome all the changes.

Subtly, each side was starting to dig in its heels on its position. In understated ways, each side resented the other. It was a reflection of what was going on in the city and our country. Now, this resentment could have gone on for a long time without much harm, so long as white families lived primarily on one side of town and black families lived miles away on the other. However, when you're meshed together in a cafeteria or a gym class, or seated next to each other in a science class, you start catching what the other person is throwing—and eventually you might be offended by it.

So a latent racial resentment was there at the

start of my final year in the Plainfield school system, beginning in September 1968. The football season, with its common goal of victory, would mask underlying feelings for the first couple of months of the year. Things were OK through Thanksgiving. December, with Christmas as the dominant theme, continued to suggest harmony. However, as the new year started, the appearance of harmony started to fade. Why exactly, I can't say. But if I had to pinpoint a stressor, a carrier of the racist virus, it might have been through PHS's primarily black basketball team that would often play all-white teams on their schedule. Suggestions of racially biased officiating during the varsity games started popping up late in January.

One more time, please allow me to remind you that we had no cell phones, Internet, or social media as we understand them today. However, there were essentially five different times during a school day to hear the latest news, gossip, and rumors. They were homeroom, before academic classes started, in the hallways, in gym class around the locker room, and in the cafeteria. Through those avenues, a buzz started around the school of racial problems. Those conversations were disquieting and started a slow build-up of uneasiness that all came to a head during the last week of February 1969, a week that was, with a great deal of irony, designated "Brotherhood Week" at Plainfield High.

Monday, February 24th.

During lunch, the cafeteria, loaded with students, seemed to be louder than usual that day. Now, I was eating with a few of my nerdy friends. I'm sure we were not talking about sports or anything like that. But I could tell that most of the students in the cafeteria were not talking about sports either. There was a strange but detectable vibe about the place. It reminded me of the time I rode my bike around the West End of Plainfield before the riot; I could just feel that something was wrong. Well, on that Monday, I could feel that something was not right there at Plainfield High School. But I couldn't define it.

Tuesday, February 25th.

The day started with a buzz that there had been a fight after school on Monday, probably along the lower levels between a black and a white student.

PHS back then was a massive, three-story brick building with a basement level that gave it a total of four floors (most of that building was torn down once the new school was completed. What's now the high school parking lot was once part of the huge building). Well, most academic classes were on the upper floors with wide, brightly-lit corridors. However, the corridors on the windowless basement level were lit only by a row of fluorescent lights. Plumbing and wiring that maintained the building were visible along many of the walls of those corridors. The smell of chlorine from the pool, also located on that lower level, was prevalent much of the time.

When it was time to change classes, many of the teachers left their classrooms and stood in the hallway by their classroom door. Their job was just to show a presence of authority while the hundreds of students moved along during changes of classes. That simple monitoring had proven to be a pretty good deterrent to bullying, horseplay, etc. However, there was hardly any monitoring along the dark lower levels, especially near the pool. If there was to be a fight, especially with no adult witnesses, that was an excellent spot. And that's where the rumored fight took place.

Wednesday, February 26th.

Wednesday morning started with more rumors of fights that supposedly took place after school on Tuesday. These "fights" were always between white and black boys, juniors or seniors, and usually the jocks. Nerds were never part of the physical racial unrest. However, sometimes, girls also got into it. Nevertheless, for the most part, it was the toughest and strongest from each side that attacked each other. The star athletes, who could do the most damage, were usually not the prime culprits. It was the ones just below them who would be the antagonists. To their credit, the star athletes would usually try to avoid or break up such brawls. They were thinking of college and their futures; they had no time or inclination for such violent foolishness.

But they weren't totally immune.

Thursday, February 27th.

Another morning started with gossip, rumors, and some facts about a fight last night between the PHS varsity basketball team and a private high school team in Elizabeth. The PHS Cardinals were mostly black, the Elizabeth team mostly white. Plainfield lost the game and the PHS players felt it was due to the referees, who were white, making ridiculous calls against them all night. People took their basketball seriously. So to have a racial scandal associated with basketball was just too much for many. That event, along with all the flare-ups during the week, caused a hostile environment in the building. The ill will was absolutely thick; I could feel it. Even the teachers looked nervous during the day. Something was going to happen and it did—after school.

For me, once that final school bell rang, I was out of there and on my way home. I made sure I had my blue bus ticket as I headed for Seventh Street to catch the city bus that would take me to Clinton Avenue and West Fourth Street. From there, I'd walk the two blocks home. That was my routine while at PHS.

But on that Thursday afternoon, I did something different.

I decided to stay after school to use the PHS library to check out a couple of books. One of my English teachers at PHS, Mrs. VanCleef, had converted me into an avid reader. Mrs. Cunningham, my fifth-grade teacher at Barlow School, had activated the writer in me. However, it was Mrs. VanCleef who had taken my interest in reading newspapers and magazines and had channeled it into a passion for reading books.

I stayed at the library until about 3:30. I left the building on the Kenyon Avenue side. As I approached the corner of Arlington and West Ninth Street, I noticed a lot of students in the area.

That was unusual.

If you stayed 30-40 minutes after school, that would pretty much guarantee that you would find very few people outside the school when you left. So then why so many students? As I reached West Ninth Street, the large crowd of students started moving to my right. That would take them along Ninth Street toward Park Avenue. I decided to follow the crowd and find out what was going on. As I approached College Place (a very small street just before Park Avenue), I noticed within the large crowd of students a parked police car.

OK, now I was really curious.

At least a hundred students were in the area. They were standing in the street (that was Ninth Street) and near busy Park Avenue. As I got closer and actually became part of the crowd, I finally found the source of everyone's attention—a fistfight. I couldn't identify the two combatants, but it was definitely a black student against a white student. Soon there was another duo fighting, then another. The whole thing reminded me of a small tornado; there was this core of people fighting and moving, and then there were the spectators, circling and moving around the fighters. Within this storm of people was one single Plainfield Police officer. He valiantly tried to wedge in between the spectator students to get to the center of the fight.

I then witnessed something that stunned me— I saw a couple of the students hit the policeman.

Now, I had seen my fair share of television over the years. In that make-believe world, cops are in fights and shot at all the time. But not in my real world. I was aware that blacks across the country had stated a host of problems with police. Studies from all the riots across the country noted that police brutality had always been part of the recipe of a riot. But as a black teenager in Plainfield, I had not seen any police brutality. Every cop I ever met treated me with civility. My excellent fifth grade teacher's brother was a cop. He came to our class and we had great fun with him. He even left a real German Luger gun, which he had captured in World War II, for us to play with (remember, it was a different time). So, he was beyond cool to us.

Even if you had a problem with a cop, you would never touch one. Hitting a cop would be like hitting a doctor or a priest—you'd never even consider it. Yet right in front of me, with my own eyes, I saw one, then two, then three students attack an officer of the law.

They kept hitting the police officer until he fell to the ground. I couldn't believe my eyes. Then the crowd went into a frenzy: some were trying to run away and others tried to run to the fight. I had decided I should go to the officer and help in some way when about a half-dozen police cars arrived along Park Avenue. Teams of cops poured into the scene. As I moved toward the center of the trouble, I stopped and thought—black kid, cops with guns, one of their own is hurt—logic dictated it was best for me to leave the scene. And I did. As I turned around and moved away from the confusion, I kept looking back to see what was going on. My internal camera was recording it all, and I was still in shock. Nowadays, everything I saw would have been posted on social media and it would have gone viral. However, I would bet there is not one photo in existence of what happened on that cold Thursday afternoon.

When I got home, I had a great story for the

family. My mother got on the phone and initiated her grapevine news service to all her friends. Much later on, I learned that the cop who was beaten was only 22 years old. His name was Stanley Dobrydnio, and he had suffered a severe concussion from the attack.

So far, "Brotherhood Week" had turned into a version of *Fight Club*.

16 THE PLAINFIELD HIGH SCHOOL RIOT

"BLACK FRIDAY"

Friday, February 28, 1969

There had been trouble all week at Plainfield High School. The episode I had personally witnessed Thursday afternoon was by far the worst of the clashes. Was that to be the end of it? I mean, there would have to be some repercussions, some punishment, probably some kids suspended from school for what had happened yesterday. Undoubtedly, Thursday afternoon's ruckus, which included injuring a police officer, would have to be the height of our troubles. Things would definitely calm down.

At least, that's what I was thinking.

But I was not adept at anticipating the

behavior of people who were angry and had a hidden agenda. Furthermore, I wasn't aware of the intensity of the forces behind the scenes on the black side and forces on the white side who were compelling young people to stand their ground. People like Linward Cathcart and other black leaders were not instigating any sort of violence. But they were certainly there, in the background, as a support unit for black students. As a matter of fact, Cathcart had started an organization called Youth for Action Movement, also known as YAM. Almost simultaneously, a support group for the white students had been created. It was called Save Our City, or SOC, and led by a person named Joe Cavallo. Members of that organization met at a place called Assunta Hall on Johnston Avenue on the East Side of Plainfield.

A few weeks after the trouble at PHS, I drove by Assunta Hall. I had lived on the East End of Plainfield when I was 12 years old. Assunta Hall was near a large playground known as Seidler Field; I played there a lot as a kid. I had four good friends who lived in that area, two of whom were twins. Do you recall that I was not aware of the racial makeup of my friends until I was in the 7th grade? Well, it was shortly after that awakening that I realized almost the entire neighborhood surrounding Seidler Field, including my friends, were Italians. However, I didn't see that as a problem; far from it. The most amiable white friends I had were Italians. They were always the most giving and generous of people. Unfortunately, things had changed since those happy days of the early 60s. The day I drove by Assunta Hall, it was surrounded by white teenage boys who all looked like they belonged to some sort of gang. And although they didn't do anything physically to me, their stares certainly signaled that I was not welcomed in that neighborhood.

So it was SOC vs. YAM.

It was my impression that SOC saw themselves as a white version of the NAACP. Their leaders were determined to support the white folks of Plainfield. From their point of view, white people built the city, owned the majority of the businesses, and created an excellent school system and a good middle class life. They saw black folks, especially after the riot, as a threat to the peace and culture that had established Plainfield. From African-inspired clothing to black music and soul food, in their minds, it all represented a threat to their peaceful white culture. And to be fair, I suppose I could comprehend their anxieties. For white folks, living in Plainfield, right up to the city riot, had been a terrific experience. And I would have to agree that, on the surface, things had become unpleasant since the surge of black protests and demands.

But that was the paradox.

I understood and sympathized with the list of

black demands that all came down to this one point—equal opportunity. Systemically, the heart of the trouble at PHS might have been the lack of equal opportunity for black students. But the short-term tactical problem was that white students didn't feel safe and black students were angry. That condition started the clashes that brought us to that ominous Friday morning.

In spite of all that, my day started as usual. Although I would take a bus from school to home, from home to school I came by way of my generous and considerate white neighbor, Mr. Connor, who drove me to school every day. Good old Mr. Connor owned a gas station in Scotch Plains. On the way there, he would drop me off at the corner of Seventh Street and Arlington Avenue right at the elegant, first-class Park Hotel (well, it was elegant and classy back then). I would get out and walk along Arlington to Eighth Street, zip through small Library Park, and arrive at Ninth Street. From Mr. Connor's car to Plainfield High School was maybe an eight-minute hike.

But something was different that morning.

At Ninth and Arlington, there was a white teenage girl handing out flyers to students. That had never happened before; I wondered what was going on. As I moved toward her, I noticed that she was giving flyers to only the white students. To any black person that approached her, she gave a hateful glare and then turned her back to them. She did the same maneuver as I walked by her. That was the first time I had personally faced racial hostility, and it wasn't pleasant. While standing there on the corner of Ninth and Arlington, I looked east in the direction of yesterday's fight. Standing over there were other white students handing out flyers to only white students. I continued along Arlington to the entrance to the building. Along the way, I saw more white students passing out flyers to other white students.

OK, what was going on?

I entered the building and went directly to my locker that was on the first floor. As I left some books and my winter coat there, I couldn't help but notice that the hallways were strangely under-populated. PHS had 1,666 students; add teachers, janitors, administrators, cooks, and other specialists, and you had almost 1,800 people that were supposed to be there. Yet, I saw only four or five students in the corridor with me. Where was everybody else? I went to my homeroom that was also on the first floor. Every day started in that room. Once the opening bell rang, like clockwork, our homeroom teacher would close the door as the loudspeaker in the room would crackle on. You'd hear a hearty good morning and then various announcements. Afterwards, maybe the homeroom teacher would have a few words. Anne K. Campolattano, or "Mrs. Camp," as she liked to be called, was terrific. She was very motherly to us and created an environment that reminded me of a cozy living room. She truly wanted to start each of our days at PHS well.

On that Friday morning, there were very few students in homeroom. Mrs. Camp was unusually stressed; she was actually wringing her hands. One of my white friends in homeroom had one of the flyers being passed outside. He let me see it. It was a call for white students only to go to an assembly being held in the PHS auditorium that Friday morning. It was not sponsored by the school at all. The purpose of the meeting was essentially to do something about the black students.

So, someone had organized a whites-only meeting to complain about black students during a week of racial clashes *and they expected it to be peaceful?* No wonder poor Mrs. Camp appeared anxious.

The bell rang and we were off to our first-period class. For me, it was a math class on the second floor. I entered the room and noticed that two-thirds of the class were missing. The teacher attempted to get into the lesson, but it was a weak effort. Everyone in that room, including the teacher, was distracted. We weren't there long when, suddenly, it felt like the building shook. That is not an exaggeration on my part. I could honestly feel a thunderous vibration shake the building for a few seconds. We all stopped our work. Within minutes of that jolt, the loudspeaker in the room turned on. We heard a frightened voice say, *"School is over for today, leave the building immediately."* I had not heard an announcement abruptly ending school since November 22, 1963 when, at Maxson Junior High School, we learned of the assassination of President Kennedy and were ordered to go home.

What had happened to cause that announcement?

Well, that unsanctioned assembly in the school auditorium had started just about the time everyone should have been in homeroom. The huge room was in the shape of a rectangle. The lower level maintained that rectangular shape. However, the large balcony was shaped like a horseshoe. The whole place looked very much like a theater in New York.

On that morning, the lower level contained only the invited white students. However, filling the entire balcony were uninvited black students who had come on their own to that assembly. The place was packed with more than 1,000 people. To my surprise, I learned that the new mayor of Plainfield, Frank H. Blatz, was there along with Dr. Noble Hiebert, the superintendent of all the Plainfield schools. Accordingly, they had been invited by the white students to speak on the need for things to settle down at the high school.

To me, the assembly just seemed wrong. If there were to be such a thing, it should have been for everyone and initiated by the principal, Wallace F. Gleason (no relationship to Officer Gleason). Since I had no conduct problems, I had never met Mr. Gleason during my years at PHS. I never even said hello to him. He was a white man, a big guy physically, but during all of those days of problems, he seemed invisible to me. I couldn't help but think that stronger leadership could have prevented the schism that was taking place in our school.

I'm not sure how that awkward assembly commenced, but I do know that within minutes of its start, two white girls, on their own accord, stood up and moved to the front stage. One or both of them said, loud enough for everyone to hear, "*All black people are pigs, and white students will not allow blacks to have superiority over them.*"

Every black and white friend I questioned afterward, who had been there, confirmed that was what the girls said. And just about then was when the building shook.

Seconds after they said that, black students in the balcony started throwing chairs down on the white students. A few of the more athletic ones actually descended over the railing from the balcony and jumped on white students. Fights started everywhere. Several furious black girls raced after the two white girls who had made the inflammatory remarks and started pounding on them. One or two policemen who had been in the school, I guess as security for the mayor, ran into the auditorium.

That's when the announcement came over the public address system.

I left my math class totally bewildered as to what to do.

The building was shaped like a giant square donut, four levels high. I was on the second floor on one side; I needed to get to the opposite side and down a flight of steps to get to my locker and retrieve my coat. It was a cold February day. I was still on the second floor as students of all colors where flying by me, but I managed to get to the other side. However, I was still on the second floor. I went through the fire door and headed downstairs, but before I reached bottom, I could see through the windows of the double doors on the first floor.

And what I saw was unbelievable.

There in front of me was a sea of people. White students, black students, and cops—all fighting each other. It looked like a scene from a TV western when there was a massive fight in a saloon. Attempting to get through that to my locker would have been impossible and crazy on my part. So I went back upstairs to the second floor. I ran around to the other side of the building looking for a safe exit. I saw my friend Tom, who was white, a few steps in front of me. He was also a senior, a well-built kid who was on the swim team. Tom didn't know I was behind him, but I followed him through the doors of an exit. I was a half-flight behind him as he reached the first-floor exit doors. Just as Tom was about to grab the handle of the door, two tall black male students walked in. The bigger of the two, without any warning or anything being said, punched Tom in the face as hard as he could. My friend collapsed to the floor. Those two left him and went toward all the trouble on the first floor. I ran to Tom. He was still on the floor, bleeding from the nose and mouth. I grabbed him and tried to help him up. But he pushed me away and yelled, "Stay away from me, all of *you* people!" Tom got up and stumbled out of the door.

I never saw him again.

I was in shock.

I ran out of the same door that Tom did and headed for Library Park. I saw students running in every direction and more police cars arriving. I caught up with several of my nerdy black and white friends. It was freezing outside, and we didn't know what to do. After a few moments, we all decided to go to the YMCA building that was several blocks away. Once there, we talked to a Marjorie

Patterson. She was the director of the youth department there. It was a position of note, considering she was a black female in an all-male staff and with an 80% white clientele. Miss Patterson was very involved in the community. Amazed by our accountings, she got on the phone and attempted to find out what was going on.

We stayed there a while, and then we decided it was best to get to our homes. Once I was warm enough, I used my bus ticket to get home. I'll never forget the mixed feelings of that day. I was in shock, I was horrified, I was disoriented, I was so mad at those guys who had attacked Tom, and I was so hurt by Tom's reaction. I was hot, and I was freezing cold.

It was the worst day I ever had at school.

******

Before the end of that Friday, the Board of Education closed every school in Plainfield and ordered that they not be opened again until the following Thursday. They felt that "timeout" would act as a cooling-off period.

Plainfield High School would be closed even longer. It would not open again until Tuesday, March 11th.

In the intervening time, the black students, led by YAM, had meetings at the Neighborhood House on the West End while the white students, led by SOC, held meetings at Assunta Hall on the East End. Each group blamed the other for the problems. And I'm certain there was a good deal of strategizing of what to do next.

One thing, I thought, was particularly unfair. I was a witness to the massive turmoil on that Friday, February 28th. Hundreds were involved, yet only one person was arrested—18-year-old Robert Nelson, a black student. Now, I have no idea if he was guilty of the charges of assaulting a police officer at the high school or not. But there's no doubt he shouldn't have been the *only* one arrested. Dozens on both sides had broken the law. But arresting only one black student helped to verify the black students' claim of an unjust system at the high school.

The students weren't the only ones who felt it wrong to essentially put all the blame of that entire fiasco on one person.

On Saturday, March 1st, more than 200 black people marched to the Municipal Court of Plainfield shouting "black power" and demanded the release of Robert Nelson. Nelson was eventually released on bail after a noisy arraignment with disruptive protests during the hearing.

Just about at the same time, a crowd of about 200 white students met at Assunta Hall. They shouted their concerns about the blacks trying to take over the high school.

There were meetings at churches, community centers, homes, and garages. Oddly, there was one note of commonality—that the high school principal, Wallace Gleason, should be fired. Now, the black students and parents were more adamant about it than the white students and their parents. However, the white groups made it clear that they did not want a black principal to replace Mr. Wallace. After all the furor, Principal Wallace did not leave PHS, but he had lost the respect from many for not showing any viable leadership during all the weeks leading up to the school riot.

Dr. Hiebert, Superintendent of Schools, and Mayor Blatz called upon teachers, social experts, community leaders, and even the clergy to help them come to some solution about the high school problem. I don't recall if they ever presented a formal plan. All I know for sure was that I got a ten-day unscheduled vacation.

******

On Tuesday, March 11th, we finally went back to school.

Good old Mr. Connor dropped me off at the Park Hotel and again I walked along Arlington Avenue to Eighth Street. Everything was normal until I reached Library Park. I will never forget what

I saw in front of me—literally hundreds of policemen, all of them wearing helmets and carrying nightsticks. I looked over to the brand-new library, and it was encircled exclusively by New Jersey State Troopers. I crossed the street and walked by the phalanx of cops. I noticed their uniforms; they were from every city surrounding Plainfield... much like they had been during the city riots. Every few feet, there was another policeman. When I got to Ninth and Arlington, there were even more police surrounding the entire high school. More than 400 cops were there to "make it safe" for us. Some of the cops smiled at me. A few even said, "Good morning, son." However, the majority didn't appear too happy at all.

Once inside PHS, there were no police, but I did see community leaders along the hallways. Oddly, with all that security and monitoring, there were relatively few students in the building. Most had stayed home. I learned later that many black students were boycotting until demands were made. And many white students (who were not aware of the planned massive show of police) didn't think they would be safe. Whatever the reasons, that first day back to school was bizarre. Little work was done. Most of us spent a lot of time looking out the windows at the army of police. We learned later that policemen were stationed at every school in Plainfield that day.

The next day, there were maybe 200

policemen, and fewer the next day. Nevertheless, there was a police presence around the school for quite a while.

Over the next few weeks, we were given identification badges, and private guards patrolled the hallways. That was the beginning of that type of security in the Plainfield school systems. And that was the only outcome I noticed from all the meetings that were held during those days.

The Courier News reported that Mayor Blatz had watched the re-opening of the high school. His comments were: "I am distressed to see the city brought to a position where we have to use police in order to ensure the safe opening of our high school. I believe this type of confrontation is unnecessary."

I met Mayor Blatz sometime later. He was a relatively young white man and a Republican. I don't think he held any prejudices against anyone. He simply wanted Plainfield to go back to its peaceful pleasant self. It was a good intention on his part, but it was also naïve. Plainfield was never going to be the same again.

17 PLAINFIELD
"THE AFTERMATH"

While I was still at Plainfield High School, our metal shop classes had a unique experience, one that I'm sure no other class has had since and probably will ever have again.

By my senior year, the high school building, although large, was very old; it was time for a replacement. So the city decided to build a new PHS near the old high school. They started by buying every house on Park Avenue between Ninth Street and Stelle Avenue. That area was known as Doctor's Row because just about every house on the street was a doctor's office and had been for years. Now that the city owned them, the houses were designated for demolition, which would allow space for a new high school. However, our metal and wood shop teachers had secured permission for all the boys' Industrial Arts classes to go over to those houses and rip out the copper pipes in the walls before demolition started.

Can you imagine that?

For one week, when it was time for us to report to class, we would instead go to our shop room to pick up a hammer or an axe or a saw— anything that could wreck things. We would then leave school and walk over to one of the former doctor's offices and rip through any wall we thought would hold a copper pipe. For the most part, we were totally unsupervised—it was wild. I never had so much fun at school. After a week of a hundred high school boys smashing through dry wall and cutting through wooden frames, the houses were actually dangerous. I almost fell through gaping holes on the floors. Nevertheless, we found and removed every piece of copper, and it raised quite a bit of money for the school. I think back at that week and realize no insurance company today would ever endorse that.

Eventually, the houses were bulldozed and the land was leveled and mapped out. Unfortunately, the architects found the ground unstable. So, to handle the weight of a new steel and concrete structure, pilings would have to be installed in the soil. So, for weeks during our senior year, our classrooms shook constantly as towering machines repeatedly dropped tons of weight on hundreds of spots creating solid ground to support a new state-of-the-art high school—that we would never see or use.

The incessant pounding of those pile drivers, the distraction and headaches they caused, well, they were symbolic of my last months at PHS and the Plainfield school system.

Oh, as a student body we did settle down. There were no more fights, at least no big ones, and no more confrontations. But there was no more fun, no more joy either (with the exception of destroying those houses). If a book dropped too loudly on the floor it caused many to jump out of their seats. The new ID badges and security guards were constant reminders that we couldn't be trusted. And because our school disturbance wasn't about sports, or politics, but race, there was now an invisible yet very evident boundary between black and white students.

Our senior prom in May was held at a place that doesn't exist anymore, "Whelan's Steak House" on Route 22 near Springfield. As I recall, it was the first time since that horrible assembly that we were all in the same room together. In spite of the difficult school year, it seemed like the entire senior class was there. However, there was a bit of tension in the air. I noticed the table seating—black couples were seated together and white couples were together. It looked like something out of the Deep South. Nevertheless, there was no trouble;

we were all just well-dressed teenagers eating steak and string beans at mostly segregated tables.

But then my date, who was a progressive young lady, walked over to a white boy, a longtime friend of hers, who was dancing with his white girlfriend. My date cut in and started dancing with the boy. As those two maneuvered around, I noticed the white girl was just standing there alone. So, to be polite, I asked her if she wanted to dance. She politely accepted. So there we were, the only integrated couples on the dance floor, as all of our classmates watched us. And I will never forget how that cute little white girl's hands were sweating so badly that they soaked right through her gloves. I felt like I was holding onto sponges. Nonetheless, without the intention, we had helped to reduce some of the pressure in that room. Before the evening was over, many blacks and whites who had been friends since kindergarten danced together.

About a month later, graduation was held. It was quiet with no incidents, although there were more police there than I think other graduations hosted.

******

The famous tragic story, *Gone with the Wind*—I had read the book and seen the movie before I could fully comprehend what that title meant. The

Southern culture of plantations, wealthy owners, pampered Southern belles and their privileged beaus, and the horrific slavery system was wiped out during the Civil War. That whole society was gone with the wind.

Well, in many ways, the idealistic, peaceful Plainfield I grew up with as a child started to disappear after the racially-motivated events I have described in this book.

Many white folks took their families, businesses, and money away from Plainfield. Large, majestic, single-family homes were too expensive to keep as they were. So they were converted to affordable two-, three-, even four-family apartments. Beautiful middle-income homes in white sections of Plainfield were being sold at very low prices; some were even abandoned. White families wanted to get their children away from the perceived danger of Plainfield. And, in truth, many black families left Plainfield too. By the mid-1980s, just about every business I grew up with in downtown Plainfield was gone. White folks from the surrounding cities, a tremendous source of income, no longer came to Plainfield to shop. They shopped in their own cities or went to the malls that were developing. The great old Plainfield stores relocated to places like Westfield or to a mall or just went out of business. One of the last to go was Dreier's Sporting Goods. The owner, Bernie Dreier, a white man, was one of the most generous and fairest people I have ever known. When he finally left, to me, that was the end of the downtown Plainfield I knew as a kid. It was truly gone with the wind.

The Plainfield schools over the years went from some of New Jersey's best to the some of its worst.

Many do not recall that where the new county building in downtown Plainfield is today, bordered by Front and Second Street, Park Avenue and Madison Avenue, was originally a profitable business section in the 50s and early 60s. Those businesses and organizations, including a big church and movie theater, were torn down in 1965 as part of a brilliant plan known as the Madison Avenue Renewal Project. Its purpose was to build new, modern stores or even a mall right in the heart of Plainfield. But the 1967 riot seriously hurt the chances of anyone investing that type of money in Plainfield. And the 1969 PHS problems certainly sealed its fate.

For almost 30 years, no new buildings of any significance were built in Plainfield. And many of the stores and businesses in the West End were never rebuilt or replaced after the riot.

The city riot also took a human toll. There was the sacrifice of Office John V. Gleason and the heartbreak of his family. However, the innocent families of those who committed the murder were also destroyed. After the riot, twelve people were indicted for killing the policeman. But after years of legal wrangling, only George Merritt, Jr. and Gail Madden were convicted for the first-degree murder of Officer Gleason. I knew Gail Madden's young children. They suffered greatly while growing up in Plainfield. Their father was out of the picture early in their lives, and after their mother's arrest, they were without parents and were known as the children of a cop killer. And I can't even begin to list all the businesses, owners, and employees of the West End who lost everything during the riot. However, I will mention one— Franky, the owner of that wonderful mom-and-pop grocery store that served the community so well. It had been totally destroyed by fire and looting. I think I was about 19 when I happened to meet Franky and his wife years after the tragedy. He had not seen me since I was a child, so it took him a few moments to recognize the six-footer who now towered over him. He told me that he and his wife were moving back to Italy. It was clear on Franky's face that he still could not understand why he was the target of such hatred. I felt it was necessary to apologize to Franky, on behalf of my family and all the people he had truly helped. I couldn't begin to explain to him why he had borne the brunt of such violence. We were both close to tears by the time we said good-bye. As he walked away in his worn-out jacket, tattered hat, and scuffed shoes, I realized that he wasn't a rich storeowner; he was a just a poor guy who had tried to make a living. That store had probably been his dream—and it was gone. I can't express to you how sad I felt as that broken-hearted man faded out of sight.

******

Everett Lattimore, who tried so hard to maintain peace and order during all the disturbances, became the first Democratic mayor in Plainfield since 1915. And he was the first-ever black mayor. But the well-intentioned and good-natured Lattimore, who strove for better education for the children of Plainfield, could not stem the tide of the "White Flight." And the white families that tried to stay, well, their kids had a hard time. By the 1980s, I was an adult with my own family. White kids who I knew through my church often shared stories of how difficult it was being white and living in Plainfield. They were now the minority. One of them told me of how he got beat up just because Rodney King had gotten beat up. Although he lived in Plainfield and tried to attend Plainfield schools, after his beating, his parents decided to send him to a private high school in neighboring Scotch Plains.

By the mid-1990s, I don't think there was one white student left in Plainfield High School.

But several things have helped to save Plainfield from a total collapse.

Former lawyer Albert McWilliams became

mayor around the turn of the century. He was determined to bring businesses back to Plainfield and give the middle-class power again. When he got Union County to build their Social Services building on that old Madison Park Renewal site—35 years after the space was cleared—it was a major revitalizing step. Mr. McWilliams, who was black and a Democrat, felt that if you bring businesses back, they pay taxes, and that would put less of a burden on individual citizens. That recovery of business has been a big help to Plainfield. So, if you go to downtown Plainfield now in the 21st century, there are many stores. They don't command the attention of the surrounding communities the way Plainfield stores used to, but they are busy and thriving.

The next big change and help has been the influx of Hispanics to Plainfield. When I was a teenager in the 1960s, Hispanics were a very small population in the city, and they were not respected by whites or blacks. Why? I have no idea; I've learned in life that people are often stupid and love to hate for no rational reason. Hispanics were not even called "Hispanics" when I was growing up. No matter what country they came from, they were all called "Puerto Ricans."

However, when I was talking to a Plainfield Police officer during Mayor McWilliam's administration, that officer declared adamantly, "If it wasn't for the Hispanics with their businesses and family ethics, Plainfield would have gone to hell long ago."

Plainfield is now at least 42% Hispanic. Reflections of their values can be seen everywhere in the city. From the school system to the downtown businesses, the Hispanic culture is firmly entrenched.

In 2002, my black next-door neighbor of 30 years moved away. They were replaced by a family who originated from El Salvador. I didn't know what to expect. But they have turned out to be the best neighbors I've ever had. In many ways, their intense family relationships and generosity reminds me of the old days of Plainfield.

Perhaps there is one other point that gives me hope for Plainfield.

I visited the Plainfield Public Library about a year ago. It was the first time in a long time, and 47 years since New Jersey State Troopers surrounded it after the school riot. I was amazed by the changes. Book areas where I used to hide and study were gone. They had been replaced by banks of computers. The children's section had been completely redone. It looked like something from a Disney movie. One thing was obvious: someone had poured a lot of money into the place, much more than the city could afford.

Plainfield still has a white population that

never left, but instead adapted to the changes and still loves and supports their home of Plainfield.

People like Dottie Gutenkauf, who in 2008 led a courageous and determined fight to save Muhlenberg Hospital, represent the stouthearted white folks who are still in Plainfield. And by the way, the fight to save Muhlenberg Hospital was fought by a mix of every race in Plainfield. It was tragic losing our hospital of more than 130 years, but it was wonderful to see all the races working together for a good common cause.

My terrific teenage grandson (who is Hispanic) and I often drive around Plainfield together. We exchange stories about our city. I'll point to places and tell him what used to be there—that his barbershop on Front Street was once the Beverly Hat Shop. The McDonalds is located where Tiny Tots Toys and Dreier's Sporting Goods stores used to be. The well-equipped, Hispanic-owned gym we go to every week on Park Avenue was once the home of a prestigious lighting company. Considering that most kids are, understandably, not interested in reliving old things, my grandson listens with patience and fascination. When it's his turn to tell me of his Plainfield, he speaks of his charter school created because the traditional schools were so inadequate. He often includes stories of gang warfare and far too many murders. I tell him that I wish more Hispanic people were part of my world back then. He tells me he's never had a white kid his age as a friend—they just don't exist in Plainfield.

Grandson and I recently went to a PHS varsity basketball game. For me, that place will always be "the new building" that I never saw as a student, but in a strange way, I felt like I had helped to build it. It was good to see young black and Hispanic players proudly wearing the Plainfield Cardinal uniform just as Billy Chambers, James Baglin, Dewayne Elmore, and Chuck Lambert had done almost fifty years before.

The Bible says, *"Above all, love each other deeply, because love covers a multitude of sins."* With that belief, I can say confidently that the new Plainfield has hope. It has the potential to reach a new era of royalty that will encompass all peoples and all races. Plainfield has survived because more people loved it than hated it. At the end of the day, I can say that I'm proud to have been born and raised in Plainfield, New Jersey.

And it is my sincere hope that my grandson will one day say the same thing.

ABOUT THE AUTHOR

Since his fifth-grade teacher crowned him the class storyteller for his ability to pen unique tales, Isaiah Tremaine has spent a lot of time writing about and studying the actions of people, especially young folks. Mr. Tremaine has had the opportunity to engage all kinds of adolescents, from 15-year-old mothers and 17-year-old murderers to Eagle scouts and Ivy League-bound valedictorians. He's been a probation counselor, social worker, scouter, grade school and Sunday school teacher, and (as his friends have put it) "a father to many." From those first-hand experiences with young people of all races, religions, and social and economic levels, Mr. Tremaine uses composites of those realities and a vivid imagination to create his fascinating stories.

45881528R00098

Made in the USA
Columbia, SC
22 December 2018